Transforming School Culture through Lesson Observation

This book sets out a three-stage programme for lesson observation showing how a collaborative whole-school approach can transform the culture of the staffroom and improve outcomes for pupils. Focusing on the emotional environment of the classroom, the relationships between teachers and pupils, and teaching and learning outcomes, it will enable schools to provide a consistent approach to lesson observation where good practice can be celebrated and shared.

Revealing the positive impact of the programme on pupils' engagement and exam results, co-operation between departments and teacher well-being, the book:

- Provides clear guidance on implementing the programme and adapting it for different contexts.
- Shows how data can be used for both Ofsted and Independent Schools Inspectorate (ISI) inspection documentation.
- Addresses key issues such as culture, staff psychological contracts, the emotional environment of the school and leadership development.

If you are looking to make real impact within your school and bring about change for the better, the three-stage lesson observation programme is the tool for you. This innovative approach brings consistency, parity and fairness to lesson observation creating a secure and safe environment in which pupils can learn and teachers can teach.

Christine Cunniffe is Principal of LVS Ascot, an independent co-ed day and boarding school. She has held positions as Head of Music/Head of Year in state comprehensive and grammar schools in Hertfordshire and Slough. Christine holds a joint honours degree in History and Music, MMus from University of Reading and MBA from University of Leicester. Christine is passionate about providing a fully inclusive education for all children in a safe and emotionally healthy environment.

GW00750220

Transforming School Culture through Lesson Observation

A Collective and Collaborative Approach

Christine Cunniffe

Routledge
Taylor & Francis Group

LONDON AND NEW YORK

First published 2022
by Routledge
2 Park Square, Milton Park, Abingdon, Oxon OX14 4RN

and by Routledge
605 Third Avenue, New York, NY 10158

Routledge is an imprint of the Taylor & Francis Group, an informa business

British Library Cataloguing-in-Publication Data
A catalogue record for this book is available from the British Library

Library of Congress Cataloging-in-Publication Data
Names: Cunniffe, Christine, author.
Title: Transforming school culture through lesson observation: a collective and
collaborative approach / Christine Cunniffe.
Description: Abingdon, Oxon; New York, NY: Routledge, 2021. |
Includes bibliographical references and index.
Identifiers: LCCN 2020057282 (print) | LCCN 2020057283 (ebook) |
ISBN 9780367196424 (hardback) | ISBN 9780367196431 (paperback) |
ISBN 9780429203664 (ebook)
Subjects: LCSH: Observation (Educational method) |
Classroom environment. | Teachers–Professional relationships.
Classification: LCC LB1027.28 .C86 2021 (print) |
LCC LB1027.28 (ebook) | DDC 370.71/1–dc23
LC record available at https://lccn.loc.gov/2020057282
LC ebook record available at https://lccn.loc.gov/2020057283

ISBN: 978-0-367-19642-4 (hbk)
ISBN: 978-0-367-19643-1 (pbk)
ISBN: 978-0-429-20366-4 (ebk)

Typeset in Palatino LT Std
by Newgen Publishing UK

Contents

Figures

Tables

Preface

Our experiences when growing up significantly influence our behaviour, attitudes and beliefs as adults. Many readers will agree that school and all that went with it consumed our lives as children and there were few experiences for many of us beyond school life. It sounds too simplistic and obvious to stress, therefore, how important schools are to a child's development, well-being and happiness, but my experiences of education and those who influenced my life either positively or negatively have played a significant part in the development of my ethos for education. This has resulted in the development of the three-stage lesson observation programme that is the subject of this book. Little has changed despite technological advance. The same problems are still apparent – they are just dressed up in a different guise. My childhood and the challenges it brought are important in explaining the at times quite emotional text within this book and the ultimate objective of the programme to ensure that the environment in which children learn is caring, safe and supportive where all children can succeed.

Born in 1967, I was brought up on one of the largest council estates in the south-east, a typical post-war semi with an outhouse. My parents had moved to this council house as a young married couple with two small children, ten years prior to my birth. This was to be my family home until I left for university at eighteen. As children, we roamed for hours in the dead-end valley and the woods that encased the estate, imprisoning it away from the more upmarket areas beyond the woods. In the house, no one ever used the front room, and you came and went by the back door, which was always open. There was no central heating and money was scarce. The estate was built with only one way in and the same road out, and many children never left, repeating the social cycle. The local primary school did not teach us solid grammar or algebra, nor any foreign languages. We played a lot outside where most of our learning took place, and this love of the outdoors and what we learned roaming the fields and woodland has helped me forge my own education agenda.

If you had told me then that I would lead a large independent school in Berkshire I wouldn't have been in awe. I didn't know that private schools existed other than from my mother's disdainful reference to her 'posh' friend's child. I had no idea of life outside the estate and lacked the middle-class exposure to expectations of education and careers that most of my peers had.

I saw how my parents were spoken down to and my father physically struck by a work colleague, and this sense of inequality and lack of inclusion has also shaped my educational ideology. Between my mother and our primary school headmaster, I was coached into a high-performing grammar school in the town. But even there we, along with other families like mine, were looked down on by teachers and other parents. In the first week we were given a questionnaire to complete which asked questions about our parents' jobs and also what newspapers they read. I remember my mother being furious with me when I got home from school as I 'should have lied'.

Our wooden desks were the statutory one metre apart, and I remember being terrified as our Latin teacher stomped slowly down the aisles, conjugating verbs. I was always at the front through no choice of my own, and I still remember the fear of her arriving behind me and her loud voice reverberating in my ear. I can still picture our history teacher, who relished reading exam results in descending order, pausing before the last, number 32: 'Guess who came last again?' I remember feeling ashamed, embarrassed and a failure, so much so that in school I started to play up slightly, and at home I became a recluse. My light went out, my confidence diminished, and at fourteen years old I felt worthless. Even my passion for playing the piano died.

With our family constantly being told that I could aspire to two O levels in religious studies and music, but possibly CSEs if the school could bring itself to stoop to the lower exam, it was time to change. They tried long and hard to get rid of me along with others who would not make the county newspaper on results day for achieving five O levels. Many children left. What it did for me, though, was make me determined. Although my mother wanted with all her heart for me to succeed at the grammar school because 'I could have gone to grammar school but my parents didn't let me', she saw the destruction it was causing.

She was a brave working-class woman who battled with the local education authority and refused to leave the building until they moved me. On being offered another slightly less prestigious grammar school, she politely told them where they could put this school and demanded a model comprehensive on the edge of town. After a six-hour sit-in she was given the comprehensive place for me, and I started a week later after the May half-term break.

I spent the rest of my education to eighteen at the model comprehensive and it wasn't too long before this wonderful school with its inspirational teachers in a fully inclusive setting relighted the fire in my eyes. Somehow my mother persuaded the owner of the Bucks School of Music to take me on for piano lessons and the distinctions rolled in all the way to Grade 8. I enjoyed every minute of my schooling, becoming head girl, and reasonably good A-level results led to a place at university – the first in our family to have further and higher education. Along the way, the school ensured we all had opportunities no matter who we were, and we tried different skills and embraced challenging opportunities to become well rounded, confident and resilient.

I use the story of my own education at prospective parents' and pupils' open day speeches and still find it incredibly emotional to speak about. After the speech about how my own experience has determined the leader I am and my philosophy for the school, many parents have the same story to tell and they want the light in their children's eyes to remain burning brightly too. Unfortunately, my experience wasn't just because it was the 1970s – it is still going on in our schools now. I talk from a mother's heart too; I have learned more about being a teacher through my children's eyes than any other forum.

I am still highly driven by my educational experiences and it was primarily the importance of creating a positive emotional environment in school that kick-started the idea of a three-stage lesson observation programme. Other factors for change included being in a staff-centred school (rather than a child-centred environment) where mediocre practices and an anti-management culture prevailed.

The three-stage lesson observation programme leaves no stone unturned. It provides a consistent and fair approach to raising teaching and learning standards, improves relationships across the school, produces a shared collective vision for excellence in a coaching and mentoring environment, and ultimately forges and creates a positive and productive culture – a vision held by all.

Introduction

This book is about a three-stage lesson observation programme that I introduced into my school in 2014. When I took up my headship in 2010, I inherited the traditional lesson observation for staff appraisal model, which brought with it suspicion, hostility and resistance to observation. It was quite hit and miss, due to the inconsistencies in expectations and practices of the heads of department who undertook the observations. They were very closed affairs and quite 'you scratch my back and I'll scratch yours' in their outcomes. Looking at the overall outcomes of the objectives, there was no way that the school was running that perfectly with regards to teaching and learning, results and, most importantly, the emotional environment in the school. Along with the appraisal and lesson observation came peer reviews, which were probably introduced in good faith by my predecessor as watered-down 360-degree review attempts; but they were completely sycophantic, fuelling the narcissism that largely prevailed throughout the teaching staff.

The key narcissists held themselves in such high regard they felt able to cause a new headteacher trouble, stirring up the common room that can bring any headteacher down for no good reason other than their desire to run the school how they wanted to. Driven by my experiences of bad behaviour from teachers, I was no longer prepared for rudeness and superiority towards the pupils and decided the time was for change. I felt as if I was being blocked from engaging with staff at all levels, and I wanted to build a trusting relationship and lay to rest the perils of the past. It was an acidic environment to work in and this culture was ingrained into the very depths of the school. As we know, the inner core of culture, the storytelling and people's perceptions of what had happened in the past, is extremely hard to dispel (Chapter 2) and until this had been dug out and re-established, the total culture of the school would never change. Culture is important because it doesn't just affect staff; it radiates to infest pupils and parents too, and these myths and misunderstandings do not bode well for good relationships and happy people. The three-stage lesson observation programme allows for open, honest, transparent sharing and exchanging of information from the horse's mouth, thereby eating away at the inner part of the cultural onion, which can be the most difficult aspect of culture to change. My initial aim was to gain a real insight into our practices, ensure consistency and fairness across the school, and build good relationships with staff – I did not foresee the knock-on effect it would have on school culture.

There is also much more to teaching effectively than the lesson itself: the quality of planning, use of resources, expectations, marking with summative and formative feedback, standards of report writing (which was dismally poor) – the list is exhausting! If one person undertakes the whole lot, unscrupulousness and bad practice can slip in; if more than one person is involved, a more genuine, holistic overall performance is achievable because we all have different opinions and expectations. However, the most important focus is on the lesson observation itself, on the ground floor, experiencing first- hand the learning environment for pupils and their outcomes.

The three-stage lesson observation programme is not linked to staff appraisal, which is a separate activity: a live, ongoing process for professional development and training. This is an effective tool where staff take ownership of their own development. Separating lesson observation from appraisal is paramount to the success of a happy and trusting staffroom and a happy school with excellent outcomes for pupils. Happy children learn better and happy staff are more productive.

Why is the three-stage lesson observation programme collaborative?

Traditionally, formal lesson observation is undertaken by a line manager, often – and despite good intentions – with fixed views regarding what good teaching looks like and not necessarily a true reflection of what is going on. The issues with one person undertaking the observation could match those above: the observer's views on what looks good are subjective and personal, and in cases where relationships may be strained can lead to allegations of favouritism or bullying. Forging a holistic school-wide picture of what is happening in the classroom is difficult.

The idea behind the three-stage lesson observation programme is that it is collaborative as a number of different staff and pupils are involved. This could be as many as a school feels appropriate. Pupil feedback is collected in each lesson and compared with teacher feedback, which opens discussion on any different perceptions of what is occurring in the classroom. Once fully implemented, staff and pupils talk openly to each other, discuss good practice and share experiences. The process is not a closed one, but one of transparency, fairness and collaborative working.

What are the objectives of the three-stage lesson observation programme?

The three-stage lesson observation programme is intended to ensure observations are impartial and that the emotional environment of the class is the most important factor in effective teaching and learning. It provides a consistent and fair approach to observation throughout the school but at the same time embraces and celebrates individuality to ensure staff feel supported. I remember seeing a programme where a person was cured of their fear of spiders by using flooding therapy; literally being smothered with the eight-legged furry friends. Apply this method to lesson observation – the 'flooding' the programme creates takes away the fear and suspicion of observation and at the same time ensures that policies and procedures, as well as whole-school expectations, become the norm and part of the fabric of the school culture. Ultimately, it creates a shared, united vision and a positive culture of trust and collaboration.

What is the three-stage lesson observation programme?

As it says on the box, there are three stages to the lesson observation process.

Stage 1: One or more lesson observations undertaken by the senior management team (SMT), heads of department (HoDs) or other teaching staff depending on the size of the school and the logistics of seeing all staff in the academic year. Dual observations in the early days while establishing the vision are effective.

The focus is on the emotional environment in the classroom. Traditional lesson observation usually focuses on pedagogy, and inspection observations focus on outcomes for pupils. What is different in this programme is that the emotional environment in the class is the most important factor.

All teaching staff are observed, and how lessons are observed will depend on where your school is on its journey. If you as leader can observe the lessons, or follow up with a visit to the class to see the emotional environment for yourself, do so: it is invaluable.

Stage 2: Within a week of the Stage 1 lesson observation, a Stage 2 meeting with a different member of SMT takes place to look at factors outside the classroom including marking, assessment, monitoring and tracking (use of data), special educational needs (SEN) and English as an additional language (EAL) information and standard of report writing.

When staff are in a one-to-one situation with SMT, it holds staff to account for these important aspects of their job to be discussed. A coaching and mentoring style meeting such as this is highly valued by staff and in some cases, where the standards are not quite met, a second meeting can take place.

Stage 3: Within a week of Stage 2, a Stage 3 meeting with the headteacher takes places to discuss Stages 1 and 2. This is a time to celebrate what has been achieved in these two stages, and a coaching and mentoring session to look at the member of staff's contribution to the co-curricular programme and to school generally. This meeting also embraces discussion on management competencies where applicable and possible whole-school projects.

No member of staff wants to sit directly in front of the headteacher with any gaping holes having been revealed in the process. This time also allows the one-to-one relationship with staff to develop in a trusting environment where they know you want them to succeed. This results in staff wanting to do their best and not let anything slip for you as headteacher and the school.

How successful has it been?

I have to be honest in that I did not see this being so instrumental in changing the culture of the school. However, the culture shifted dramatically in under two years. The school went from planned, scheduled observations to unannounced observations where staff are keen to share their classes with management; where children are excited about you being in the class and where you can see the excellent relationships between teachers and pupils.

What was the impact for my school?

Six years on, we have an open, transparent culture of shared good practice and gone are the days of fear. Before the programme started, the classroom was a protected space in an environment of suspicion and fear. Now I hear laughter and fun throughout the school where pupil and staff want to be and achieve their full potential. After all, we are all on a continuous journey of learning and improvement, and how better to do it than in a supportive, trusting and nurturing environment where we can all be brave and courageous.

We as a school know where we are and what we need to do to move to the next stage of excellence. The programme has enabled us to have a very good grip on the academic side of our school, and we predicted accurately the outcomes of our ISI inspection in April 2019, including the recommendations which were not discussed with inspectors during the inspection. So embedded is the Stage 1 lesson observation programme that staff warmly welcome visitors to the classroom and are quick and passionate about offering colleagues support and advice. Such is their enthusiasm, we have another problem now in that doors cannot be wedged open because of fire regulations! The trust we have allows staff to take risks and try new things as well as improve the best learning outcomes for pupils.

Stage 2 led to a dramatic improvement in the standard of report writing and meeting deadlines. Marking, which had been an issue picked up in the ISI inspection in 2011, improved drastically. Although the meetings are fully supportive, there is nothing more uncomfortable than being in a one-to-one situation and having to explain why part of your job has not been done as required. Staff are more readily using data to inform their teaching and learning, and proving progress of all pupils.

The impact of Stage 3 is that as head I can get to know my staff. They have an opportunity to talk to me, tell me their ideas and look at the magnificent work they do. I do not pry into their lives, but many will tell me about their children, their parents and other personal challenges. These productive conversations allow flexibility where flexibility is due, time to nurture where nurture is needed, and staff appreciate being understood.

No matter where a school is in its journey to achieve this, the programme can be modified and adapted to suit individual needs. When we started in 2014, I did not foresee such rapid advancement, especially with the unannounced lesson observations and I never intended or foresaw that the impact could result in such organisational change in culture.

▍Understanding your school culture

School cultures are unique and extremely varied. In my teaching career I have seen highly unionised common rooms where a consultation would be needed to change the brand of coffee and where the head couldn't take a step forward without constant challenge. On the other hand, some school cultures are extremely positive, friendly and open to change. The themes in the book are therefore to help heads and school leaders self-reflect and understand where they are positioned and why, how, and when to move forward. It is not as simple as plonking down a new dictat to staff in the form of new lesson observation forms but understanding the wider circle of management practices to enable its success – not only in its implementation but in its development over time.

About this book

This book explores what the three-stage lesson observation is about and how it helps readers to adopt the programme or similar into their schools.

Part 1 of the book starts by reflecting on what observation is and then explores our understanding of school culture, the psychological contract and the importance of a healthy and positive emotional environment in the classroom.

Part 2 of the book provides an overview to the three-stage lesson observation programme, and then dedicates chapters to each stage, its purpose, objectives and practicalities. What preparation is needed and how do you convey the vision?

Part 3 of the book looks at wider issues around how well you know your school, yourself and your team. Do you know them well enough to effectively implement change, and how do you implement your vision?

Part 4 of the book explores how the data and information gathered during the three-stage programme can be used to build the self-evaluation form. It also considers how this will work in the 'new normal' for education following COVID-19.

There are so many facets to organisational behaviour that putting the chapters in a logical sequence was quite difficult. Part 3 could be read first as it explores all aspects of leadership, understanding ourselves and our schools before identifying possible change and what those changes are. There are useful exercises leadership teams can undertake in preparation for the culture change that the three-stage lesson observation brings. Each part of the book provides a particular function and although best read in sequence they can be revisited in any order to provide clarity and direction for implementing the programme in your school.

Part 1

What lesson observation is and current attitudes to it

This chapter explores what lesson observation is, its purpose and general attitudes towards it. This chapter explores the backdrop to traditional lesson observation practice and why it needs to change.

So what exactly is lesson observation? Technically, it is an opportunity for a teacher to be observed by another member of staff to get feedback on their practice in order to develop and grow. In reality, lesson observations are often not warmly received and can be seen as a threat with opportunities for misuse. It is important to understand how lesson observations are currently viewed and used in order to put the three-stage lesson observation programme into perspective and identify how different it is from the one-off snapshots of traditional practice.

A fear of being observed

I remember my first lesson observation, after qualifying as a teacher in 1994, was actually during an Ofsted inspection when I worked in a challenging comprehensive school in Stevenage. I can remember pulling into the car park on the first day of the inspection and feeling physically sick with nerves.

Looking back, I think I must have bored the inspector senseless; being part of a 1.5-teacher music department and there being a dedicated music specialist on the team, the poor man sat through my lessons hour after hour. On reflection, though, I feel sorry for him rather than myself: my teaching was boring. Boring because of the absolute fear

I had of the accountability placed at my feet as a new teacher in the position of Head of Music. My lessons that week were not typical in that I had planned listening-related lessons to the nth degree because I couldn't trust the pupils to do a practical lesson. This was a school where pupils routinely jumped out of windows to chat with pupils next door. In the plaster wall of the temporary building where music was taught, the imprint of a pupil who had launched himself at it the week before spoke volumes about the challenges we had. It wasn't just a lack of trust in the pupils – with water running down the walls, one keyboard and a few drums between 35 pupils, practical work was always a mighty challenge itself.

Although the school was a nice place to be, I was left alone, never observed or mentored, and Ofsted was something to be feared and not embraced. Created in 1992, Ofsted represented a new regime and the first inspections took place in 1993 to drive up standards. In my first year of teaching, I was unaware that I was technically in my probation year and yet I never had a meeting with a senior member of staff and didn't complete any paperwork, unlike the current system. Without a doubt, if I had taught in this way in the present system, the best scenario is that I would be on capability procedures, and worst case: fired!

Back then, and even today, there is widespread fear of being observed. Often linked to annual appraisal, probation, quality assurance, identifying underperformance and assessment that reports as judgements (Gosling 2005), lesson observations are the single highest cause of disputes and grievances in the sector, with reports of bullying and favouritism among managers (Allen 2014). The most significant issue of observations in the past has been the one-off planned observation that has resulted in over-planning, which is time-consuming and a false snapshot of the learning experience for pupils. Pete Smith in the Guardian of 24 July 2013 likens one-off observations to the smell of fresh paint in a hospital when the Queen is about to visit (Smith 2013).

The problem with traditional lesson observation is that the title 'lesson observation' itself breeds fear. With anything we do, while we are being watched we are conscious that someone is making judgements about what we are doing, which is very personal; and the essence of human nature is to feel wounded and threatened by judgement. It takes a person with a very thick skin not to be affected by scrutiny. Traditionally, there has always been a motive for lesson observation and it usually has had negative connotations.

What's the problem?

Association with appraisal or teacher training

Schools have different ways of undertaking lesson observations, but they are normally associated with appraisal or teacher training. Usually booked in advance, the lead-in time to an observation can be an extremely anxious time for the teacher. The amount of planning that goes into the planned observation is nonsensical. It's not a special occasion and surely the same amount of angst and planning should be put into every lesson. I remember a very irate teacher literally attacking a line manager for cancelling a lesson observation when she had put so much work into it! One lesson on its own and out of context does not show a true representation of what is going on in the classroom. Not only does the observer know this, the teacher does and so do the pupils. As part of the three-stage lesson observation programme, pupils are given feedback forms including the question, 'Is this a typical lesson?' I can assure you the response to this for the first round of the three-stage lesson observation programme will be overwhelmingly 'No'. So a member of staff may receive some good feedback from the snapshot lesson, but what happens now? Is it a case that the box is ticked and no further activities, projects or INSET happens? Are good practices shared and developed as a department, or noted and then filed away? What good comes out of traditional lesson observation? How flawed is the process?

Staff experience

The workload, angst and opportunities for abuse in the system are hot topics for unions and those more militant staff in the common room. There is an unprecedented amount of negativity in online forums and in staff bodies generally, and very little positive is seen in the traditional process. There is much dissent towards and ridicule of senior leaders, which would not be tolerated in corporate life and many other businesses. There is a vicious circle of antiquated and mismanaged lesson observation procedures that cause grievance and distrust, fuelling further 'them against us' scenarios. I carried out a survey as part of the research for this book to gain an insight into attitudes towards lesson observations and included a comments box to gather qualitative feedback. Although the responses were quite limited, I was taken aback by some comments including a statement that lesson observations were morally and ethically wrong. Online forums don't really get much better, with a tremendous amount of negativity and senior management slating.

Maybe it is just the negative teachers taking the opportunity to moan but it doesn't make good reading for those on the outside, especially the apparent bad relationships between staff and management in schools.

Although unions are trying to protect their members – and rightly so against bad and unscrupulous management practices – the shop-steward culture of the 1970s and 1980s is still prevalent in some of them. In their attempts to dictate how many hours a year a teacher should be observed, the notice period before an observation, as well as what the process should consist of, they are sending negative connotations regarding the value of lesson observations, which adds momentum to the vicious circle. How many other professions would be restricted in how often they observed the work of their employees to ensure standards and compliance?

Observations linked to appraisal are normally carried out by a member of staff more senior to the teacher being observed – normally a head of department. The focus of the lesson observations would be centred around pedagogy, content, activities and pupil outcomes. Like any exam, based on a one-off judgement, it is only natural that a member of staff is anxious and will not enjoy the experience. Add in a line manager with an unpleasant disposition, and a school culture of bullying and unfair practice – the experience can be short of terrifying.

The purpose of the three-stage programme

By having three stages the observation programme communicates to staff that time and care is being given to them to coach and mentor staff through what they are already doing and what could happen next, really focusing on the learning environment. Through a consistent approach to observation and subsequent discussions across the school, a holistic picture of what is happening can be determined and staff can be directed towards other good practices across the school, promoting collaborative working between departments. With this programme, staff know that everyone is going through the same process, with the same people, and they can feel reassured that their experience is no better or worse than the next member of staff. By the time the second cycle of the three-lesson observation starts, staff know what to expect and have a shared vision of what the school is trying to achieve. Soon, the process becomes firmly embedded into the culture of the school. The three-stage lesson observation programme takes away the fear of observation and allows for meaningful staff development that improves teaching and learning.

Who can observe lessons?

Traditionally, lesson observations are carried out by heads of department or senior managers as part of performance appraisal (here, for me, lies the problem). All staff should have the opportunity to share good practice, although the time constraints of heavy timetables often do not facilitate this, and newly qualified teachers (NQTs) have a requirement to observe their own and other departments (this is great and not a problem). Forward thinking and proactive staff will seek out other members of staff who may be particularly good at one aspect of teaching, such as behaviour management, to improve and compare their own performance – but not all staff embrace this opportunity. Good practice such as peer observation should be part of the teaching and learning culture of the school. What the three-stage lesson observation programme promotes is that whoever undertakes the lesson observation as part of this programme is clear that it is not linked to appraisal, and the focus is on the emotional environment of the school. Ideally, the headteacher or senior manager should undertake this observation to gain a holistic view of the emotional learning environment in school.

In conclusion

Lesson observation practice in its traditional form just doesn't work. No one should be fearful of being judged in any part of their work but instead be celebrated. Teachers have the subject knowledge through their degrees and teaching qualifications and have all been through a robust probationary period. We should take excellent teaching and knowledge as read and focus on what really matters: a healthy emotional environment where learning is vibrant, inspiring and celebrated.

Schools all have different cultures. You would hope all have a good learning culture of openness and shared good practice – but not all do. If you want to change the learning culture of your school, where do you start? What does your current school culture look like and what would you need to go through to get it where it should be? What are your obstacles and how do you chip away at resistance to forge a positive learning culture across the school?

What is school culture?

This chapter explores what culture is, what school culture looks like, and how we can identify our school culture.

Can you identify the culture of your school? Certainly, during the interview process we get a feeling of whether we would fit into a school – a place where we feel we belong. But how do you measure it and decide whether it needs changing? If an internal promotion, you know the devil you are dealing with, but if an external promotion, when do you really find out? Identifying your school culture, what it is, what it stands for and whether it works for what you want to achieve is an important step in establishing a collaborative culture.

Once you have identified your school culture and what you want to achieve you can use the three-stage lesson observation programme as a tool to help establish cultural change. This chapter explores organisational culture, theory behind it, the importance of culture and how to plan change.

A little background to organisational culture

Interest in organisational culture really took off during the 1980s, primarily due to the economic success of Japanese organisations. Japanese organisations had committed workers and were highly profitable, seemingly as a direct consequence of this strong culture. As a result, research surrounding organisational culture gained momentum, and studies revealed that it had a direct impact on productivity, efficiency and profitability. The research also revealed that Japanese companies operating outside Japan and with non-Japanese workers were still highly effective and threw into question national culture as a determining factor (Linstead et al. 2004). The rise of literature in this area coincided with the emergence of human resource management (HRM) and within this department predominantly lies the responsibility of organisational culture. This will become more apparent and understandable as this chapter progresses, explaining the tangible and intangible HRM processes that shape employee behaviour. Some argue that organisational culture cannot be managed and that it is not something an organisation *has* but what an organisation *is* (Smircich 1983), and some argue that management of organisation culture is key to successful innovation (Marshall 1993). 'A leader creates the vision for the culture of the organisation. That vision serves no purpose if not embraced, internalised and expressed by its members'. (George et al. 1999; p 557).

Lesson observation in the right format can serve as an effective HRM practice to move and change the culture of the organisation.

Defining organisational culture

> Organizational culture is a pattern of basic assumptions – invented, discovered, or developed by a given group as it learns to cope with its problems of external adaptation and internal integration – that has worked well enough to be considered valid and, therefore, to be taught to new members as the correct way to perceive, think, and feel in relation to those problems.
>
> (Schein, cited in Francesco and Gold 1998; p 126.)

There are an extraordinary amount of definitions attempting to pinpoint exactly what it is. However, they all have common themes, in that culture refers to the beliefs, perceptions, relationships, attitudes, and written and unwritten rules that shape and influence all aspects of how an organisation (or, in this case, school) functions (Owens and Steinhoff 1989). Another common theme is that organisational climate influences the behaviour of people in an organisation (Forte 2011) and that the relationship is a cyclical chain in that the behaviour of people affects the organisational climate/culture but in turn, the climate/culture influences the behaviour of people (Choudhury 2011).

Defining school culture

According to Purkey (1990) (cited in Higgins-D'Alessandro and Sadh 1998), each school is created by a particular combination of people in a school at any given historical point and, thus, each culture is unique. School culture is always greater than the sum of the individual contributions, and schools exhibit commonalities around set issues. Hofstede et al. (2010) state that even though there are differences among individuals, there is structure in the variety that can serve as a basis for mutual understanding. This could be likened to British culture. Although we can all safely say that we do not rely on bacon butties, fish and chips, Sunday roasts and football, most British families will still exhibit many shared values and traditions, such as the great British cup of tea (according to the UK Tea and Infusions Association, over one hundred million cups are consumed every day in the UK), bringing commonality to our communities no matter how diverse.

Focusing directly on schools as organisations, Higgins-D'Alessandro and Sadh (1998) believe that school cultures can:

1) Be separated for other aspects of schooling and operationalised.
2) Be multifaceted, in that different groups within the school experience different cultures that can overlap (Erickson 1987).
3) Meaningfully relate to students' attitudes and significantly predict students' performance, satisfaction and involvement with school.

Schools with straightforward structures, such as stand-alone independent schools or maintained schools, will possibly only see the subcultures within academic departments, especially if a large school. Having taught in three large schools, I am still surprised that some departments are unaware of staff in other departments or the work they do. Cultures within the departments, perhaps owing to the nature of the academic field of study, can be very different, and this can be celebrated rather than criticised. Although these subcultures are created informally, a well-managed, positive subculture can be a haven for innovation rather than stifled by whole school processes. Subcultures, if positive, can also strengthen the overall culture of the school. However, powerfully negative subcultures can undermine management. Sometimes organisational cultural change entails tackling only one powerful subculture to change the whole school culture, and this is where effective HRM processes are useful in sending messages that negativity and undermining will not be tolerated.

The biggest challenges with organisational culture may well lie with those schools that are part of a multi-academy trust (MAT), and more so with a school or group of schools owned by venture capitalists or part of another form of umbrella organisation. This is not always the case and very much depends on the objectives of the umbrella organisation. I have seen examples of clusters of schools where individual cultures are nurtured, and also examples where there is a one-size-fits-all approach in order to increase the bottom line. However, this conflict can also be in stand-alone schools where the objectives of governors and trustees are equally at odds with the headteacher. Headteachers can have a pretty lonely and frustrating existence with the constant demands of managing above and below. When establishing a school culture it is so important to assess who effectively owns the school and what the school is for (Sarason 1971).

Can you escape culture?

No group of people can escape culture. Groups of people thrown together in bizarre circumstances will find that norms have to be established and agreed, and a shared vision prevail, and even though there are differences among individuals, there is structure in the variety that can serve as a basis for mutual understanding (Hofstede et al. 2010). As an extreme example, the Uruguayan Air Force flight 571 that was flying members of a college rugby team and their relatives from Uruguay's capital Montevideo to Santiago, Chile, for a rugby game crashed in 1972. After nine days, with no rations left and no natural forms of food in the environment such as wildlife and foliage, the group's collective vision and mission – survival – resulted in the decision to eat the flesh of the dead passengers. Bearing in mind the passengers, dead and alive, were team mates and relatives, and predominantly Catholic in faith, they had to unlearn their traditional values and behaviours and become cannibals in order to survive. The new culture within the group resulted in their rescue two months later.

How can you identify culture?

McGrath and Bates (2013) in their handy *The Little Book of Big Management Theories* list Handy's model, Deal and Kennedy's risk and feedback model, Morgan's organisational metaphors, Graves' cultural leadership theory, Johnson and Scholes's cultural web, Hofstede's six cross-organisational dimensions, Hargreaves's balkanised cultures, and finally, but not least, Schein's three levels of organisational culture. I have cited Schein's model last as being the main focus of identifying organisational culture in this chapter based on three levels of beliefs.

1. **Artefacts and symbols:** Visible and observable, material elements of an organisation to staff and external bodies. This could be architecture, furniture, marketing materials and ceremonies. Very easy to

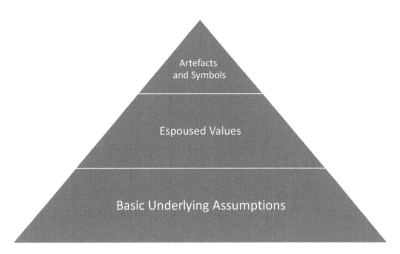

Figure 2.1 Schein's model (1985)

      change if you have the capital to change surroundings and invest in material, tangible goods and communications

2. **Espoused values:** Values and principles, rules, expectations. Harder to change as takes more thought into auditing current practices and behaviours, identifying key changes and implementing new values. This not only takes money but also a collective, managerial board-level vision with complete buy-in, and strategic, well-qualified staff in key areas to implement change

3. **Basic underlying assumptions:** Feelings, perceptions, thoughts, storytelling, myths and legends. It could be extremely hard to shake off negativity despite significant capital and human investment into areas 1 and 2. Depending on the longevity of staff, old mud sticks, such as any previous fraud, immoral and unethical behaviour on the part of a senior leader, or a bullying culture. Even harmless banter can be damaging but the long-suffering and wronged can be silent saboteurs.

All the models are useful but as Schein (1985) states, although any group's culture can be studied at three levels, it is vital that the basic underlying assumptions are deciphered to understand how to interpret the artefacts and give credence to the espoused values. The central issue for leaders is to understand the deeper levels of culture, assess the functionality of the assumptions made at that level, and deal with the anxiety that is unleashed when those assumptions are challenged. This can only be achieved through an understanding, observations and dialogue with workers.

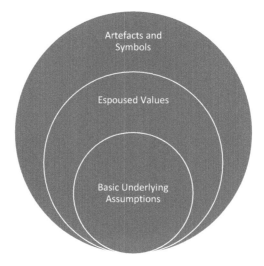

Figure 2.2 Schein's model 'onion'

For this reason, the model is also known as the onion model in that the inner core of basic underlying assumptions is the most difficult to infiltrate, understand, interpret and change.

Shein's cultural model (1985) in practice

An organisation with a strong culture will have a clear vision, clear values and beliefs, and a mission statement which is transmitted effectively throughout the organisation. Although a non-educational environment, the strongest organisational culture I have seen was at Yellow Pages during the 1990s.

> I worked in the corporate sales department, working on the special featured parts of the Yellow Pages for associations such as the Association of Chartered Certified Accountants (ACCA), the Law Society and the Federation of Master Builders. This was a part-time job while studying for my MMus at Reading University, and anyone who has ever sold advertising space, often cold-calling potential customers, will know what a thankless task it can be. This was, however, a tremendous experience in an organisation that I feel had nailed its culture. Bearing in mind I had no emotional ties or ambitions within the organisation, the investment into the communication of the vision was tremendous and it worked. I was hugely committed to reaching and often

exceeding sales targets because of the collective vision. Despite being a separate company from BT after its privatisation in 1984, sectors of the business remained close, hanging on to the family environment, and mutual respect among workers prevailed. The collective culture had been maintained and no harmful subculture had emerged.

How did they create this culture?

In 1991 the company relocated to brand new offices in Slough, leaving an old 1960s-feel office environment reminiscent of the Lionsgate series Mad Men. The furniture, branding and external visual company identity messages were evident to both internal staff and the external community. Transmitting the vision was constant, made through regular bulletins and training exercises about the best possible way to sell but truly believing that the product was worth every penny. At least every other month, the whole sales department would be transported by coach to a hotel venue somewhere and treated to a corporate day out, enjoying free lunch and drinks interspersed with sales talks and motivational speakers. Rewards were regular and celebrated, and generally this was a hugely successful and enjoyable place to work. Yellow Pages continued to be printed until January 2019, its online pages and app were used eighty million times in 2015, and it currently lists almost three million businesses. I am not surprised.

Taking into consideration Shein's model of organisational culture, one can see the characteristics in this model and that espoused values are the HRM practices of an organisation. They bridge the gap and glue together the fabric of buildings and tangible assets to the intangible and often emotional vulnerabilities of human beings in the basic underlying assumptions. HRM practices such as a code of conduct, mission statement, appraisal system, and clear messages transmitted through recruitment and induction processes, rewards and sanctions, and rites and rituals are the jam in the sponge, forming the crucial psychological contract.

1. **Artefacts and symbols:** A new office building, new furniture in corporate colours, pleasurable staff common room space, corporate identity, clear processes. Obvious to internal staff and external viewers.

2. **Espoused values:** The company had clear documented processes and procedures, rewards and sanctions, a code of conduct for boundaries and expectations of behaviour. Clear strategy, objectives and collective philosophy.
3. **Basic underlying assumptions:** Unchanged and unchallenged word-of-mouth traditions: 'how it works around here'. Embedded loyalty to the organisation through storytelling, witnessing of promotions and the tone of voice and generic message of all staff. CEO was visible, charismatic and attentive – employees felt valued.

A positive culture can take years, if not decades to establish and become the fabric of an organisation. People buy into culture; not just employees but investors. Cultural damage can happen very quickly; for example, one only has to look at the recent issue with Ken Fisher's comments at the Forbes Global CEO conference in San Francisco in October 2019 to see how behaviours of a CEO can affect assets overnight. (Mercado 2019). No matter how hard one might protest that comments were taken out of context, without doubt this will be a story told long into the future. The storytelling of these comments will be long-lived and part of the core basic underlying assumptions of the company. The same can be said of school leaders who do not lead ethically and morally. A misdemeanour on the part of leadership can have long-lasting damage which is hard to shake off. Examples of this could be anywhere from criminal activity to unfair practices that will reverberate for many years. No matter how much money you pour into the outer two layers, damage to the basic underlying assumption inner core of the onion model takes years to repair – if it ever can.

It's easy to see the culture of a company when you're in it but what follows is an example of observing a cultural shift in a company in a short space of time as a customer rather than employee.

Over the past year, a renowned country club I am a member of underwent a change of management from one brand to another with significant changes. As a member and outside pair of eyes, the two companies are equally effective, comparable and provide(d) a good product and service I was happy with. The cultural shift was interesting and, again, a good example of the Shein's model of organisational culture. With any change, one should ask why the change is happening and who the change is for. The club seemed financially buoyant and the model appeared to work, so why mend what's not broken? The changes that took place were potentially risky but with no direct competitor for a number of miles, risks were lowered. As an outsider not necessarily talking directly to staff it was evident to see the reasonably quick cultural shift that ensued.

1. **Artefacts and symbols:** The club installed a new dining room and bar layout including furnishings and new menus. The gym was revamped, an outdoor pool was installed and upmarket spa and beauty facilities abolished in favour of more class exercise space. The strong change in message was attractive to new thirty- and forty-something clientele and less popular with the older generation, especially the hike in annual fees and the couple of pence added to the price of a coffee.
2. **Espoused values:** New staff uniform; pay schemes with bonuses; employee incentives such as employee of the year; a mission statement with reinforced messages to customers and staff through bulletins and training, members meetings and other regular communication. The best thing I have seen is that rude behaviour from members is no longer tolerated, with members being refused service or their membership suspended.
3. **Basic underlying assumptions:** Despite the change being initially quite negative for staff and members, mainly because of how people receive change, the influx of new members, the clear messages and transactional relationship, and the positive storytelling all contributed to increased membership and happy staff and customers.

If you don't know the culture you are dealing with or do know the culture and want to change it, use Shein's model to assess the three layers and where the gaps lie. I would guess that in established schools with strong traditions the underlying basic assumptions will be the most interesting area to explore through conversations and observations – and more than likely the most difficult to change despite tremendous effort in the upper two layers. The three-stage lesson observation programme, through all three stages, allows you as headteacher to gather data, gain the overall picture and change staff's perceptions and realities.

The onus is on you as leader to lead by example and live by the fundamental messages of the culture of the school, which sends the strongest communication and transmission of the school's ethos, aims and vision.

> The communication of culture succeeds when the leader's values, beliefs, and standards of behavior appear in the entire fabric of the organization and to the extent that followers teach the culture to others. (George et al. 1999: p 558)

Abuse of culture

The historical abuse investigations against many educational institutions including music schools and faith schools are very much in the public eye through the current Independent Inquiry into Child Sexual Abuse (IICSA). School cultures, especially in specialist environments, can and have led to the misery of many children. The report on Ealing Abbey and St Benedict's School, which forms part of the English Benedictine Congregation case study of the Roman Catholic Church investigation, is distressing and the account of thirty years of a culture of sexual abuse is heartbreaking to read. The abusers continued their crimes shielded by the artefacts and symbols of being under the umbrella of the Roman Catholic Church and the messages, values and beliefs of the espoused values of the church. It is unbelievable, though, that some staff knew what was going on, as well as some parents, and the evidence was so clear with enough storytelling in the basic underlying assumptions that authorities failed to recognise that children were at risk. This has also been the case in many organisations, most notably in the Jimmy Savile case and the Weinstein scandal.

In conclusion

We are in a new age, with tighter regulations and inspection regimes. As headteacher, you are ultimately responsible for the culture of the your school and you have the ability to change it. The three-stage lesson observation programme is an excellent means of introducing something new and innovative, non-traditional and collaborative.

As headteacher or senior leader, do you feel a positive and productive learning environment? Children who want to be in school and staff who are passionate about delivering the best education to those children? Are pupils and staff positive and happy, and do they learn in an environment of awe and wonder? What is the emotional environment temperature in your school?

An ideal school culture is one of freedom of thought and the space, time and authority to try new practices and not fear failure. A positive school culture is one of being able to take risks and individualise learning by being able to go off-piste, by being innovative, creative and inspiring. Pupils will thrive in a happy and supportive classroom and will be excited to explore their learning and develop new skills. The three-stage lesson observation programme promotes individuality; although consistent, it is not one-size-fits-all, allowing teachers to be themselves, happy in their own skin, and this happiness will reverberate through the school community. The affirmation all staff will feel from their direct communication with senior leaders and the headteacher will give everyone the confidence to create a dynamic and forward- thinking learning environment that ultimately produces excellent outcomes for pupils.

Staff – new staff in particular – buy into the culture of the school and start their psychological contract with school from the moment they see the advert. Why is the psychological contract so important? This is explored in the next chapter.

CHAPTER 3

The psychological contract

This chapter explores what the psychological contract is, why it is important to understand and be conscious of, and how it can be nurtured to maintain positive school culture and instil trust and belief in the school. Implementation of the three-stage lesson observation programme promotes the importance of the psychological contract and in turn strengthens and nurtures school culture.

From the moment a prospective applicant views the advert for a job in the school, their psychological contract with the organisation and the school leader begins. All the messages conveyed through the advert, job description, school website and reputation of the school, including its apparent culture to the outside world form the start of a bond both tight and fragile – it needs nurturing.

What is a psychological contract?

Conway and Briner (2005) cite many definitions for the psychological contract, and generally there appears to be a lack of consensus on the definition (Suazo et al. 2011). 'A psychological contract is a set of beliefs regarding mutual obligations between employee and employer' (Robinson and Morrison 1995). Social exchange can be traced back to Adam Smith's *The Theory of Moral Sentiments* (1759) and occurs in all aspects of life. Individuals enter into an exchange because they perceive that the other party in the relationship has something to offer or contribute (Tekleab and Chiaburu 2011).

Why is it important?

The recruitment of teaching staff is an annual costly exercise and the key reasons for staff leaving, as described by Minarik et al. (2003), can be addressed more effectively if the psychological contract that develops and changes at key times during employment (George 2009) is consciously managed by the use of effective human resource management (HRM) practices often carried out by the headteacher. If employees perceive they are being treated fairly and transparently, and supported by clear and well-communicated policies and procedure, this will help the psychological contract remain intact (Blancero et al. 1997). I am focusing on the subject of the psychological contract because it is this relationship that drives a successful lesson observation programme and in return transforms school culture. A successful psychological contract breeds trust and confidence in the person who is driving the programme. The importance of Stage 3 in the lesson observation programme cannot be underestimated. 'Principal–teacher relationships offer a prime organizational case where relational trust likely develops from emotional bonds' (Price 2011:40).

The psychological contract

The psychological contract needs to be continually evaluated and nurtured to ensure continued commitment and that staff feel their contributions to school life are reciprocated. The Stage 3 meeting with the head gives an opportunity to gauge the balance in the relationship and increase the emotional bond with the employee. Teachers, on the whole, and despite me having heard stories of teachers refusing to participate in activities after school, contribute far more beyond the factual content of the material contract, and this should be formally recognised. Elstad et al. (2011) state that teachers need to be part of and loyal to the school in which they work, and commitment is related to job satisfaction and organisational citizenship behaviour (OCB). 'Teachers can withstand a great deal of stress when they feel their efforts are appreciated' (Brown and Roloff 2011:471). Teachers generally start out making a good job of learning their art and at the same time being socialised into the cultural norms of their school. To maintain this enthusiasm and commitment, employers (headteachers) need to understand what constitutes their employees' psychological contract and where in the employment journey it can go wrong (Brown and Roloff 2011). Kwan (2009) identifies six key times where the psychological contract can wrong, and George (2009) highlights five points; both identify early points, such as pre-employment, recruitment and early socialisation stages, but George also states that, as well as the contract changing over time, the psychological contract itself is often not realised until there is a breach. The one-to-one meetings in Stage 3 are a useful way for a head to monitor the temperature of individuals, as well as departments and other pockets of influence across the school.

The psychological contract is often formed with line managers and not the head and this can be potentially dangerous to the culture of the school. Without wanting to sound autocratic and a control freak, to protect the overall vision and culture of the organisation the contract also needs to lie between you as headteacher and the member of staff too. Schools can become unpleasant places to be, with a them-and-us culture of distrust (Minarik et al. 2003), and no matter how highly we regard our middle management, it doesn't take long for one or two silent saboteurs to create endemic damage. It is natural for people to discuss, assume, gossip and speculate, and therefore one-to-one contact from the horse's mouth quashes any potential trouble. Call me cynical, but when I started my headship in 2010 I inherited a wasps' nest. Lesson observation was attached to appraisals – appraisals that were generally boosted by sycophantic peer references and the culture generally: one of suspicion and mistrust driven by a small group of influencers. At the end of my first year when I read some of the comments in the formal appraisals, I was quite taken aback at the level of dissention, and it was obvious these comments had not been challenged previously. There was no apparent one-to-one discussion of these anti-management statements. That was job number one: be prepared to put your money where your mouth is. A big part of headship is being brave!

Implementing the three-stage lesson observation programme is quite intrusive, especially in those school communities where the trust has yet to be built. The psychological contract of the individual will also vary according to personality and career type, and there is an added complication. In the teaching profession there have always been strained relationships between employers and employees, and the relational psychological contracts teachers hold are normally with the students (Minarik et al. 2003). In the independent sector, there is also the added complication that the head is fundamentally running a business, and teachers often do not value the significance of this complication, especially if coming from the state sector. It is often difficult for teachers to understand that the corporate behaviour of headteachers does not stop them wanting the best for the children – they just have to bring in the money to ensure it can happen.

Some staff will be more 'precious' in their judgement of the psychological contract than others. Conway and Briner (2002) cite an employee whose psychological contract was broken within days of starting the school because his teacup went missing from the staffroom.

In conclusion

The successful fulfilment of the psychological contract of employees (teachers) in the UK can have only one outcome: the rewarding experience children have in school and the results they ultimately achieve. Fulfilment of the psychological contract correlates with high levels of OCB, which in return positively correlates to the achievements of its students (Elstad et al. 2011).

Therefore, use Stage 3 meetings to build on the psychological contract between you and the member of staff. It is extremely powerful in forging staff loyalty and your understanding of each other. Loyal staff will want to tell you what they feel is going on and what they feel uncomfortable with. Listening carefully helps build the picture of what is going on in your school.

By developing relationships with staff that are positive, trusting and supportive, staff will feel happy and confident to exude that happiness and confidence in the classroom. Being made to feel safe to be yourself and show warmth, compassion and understanding in the classroom forges the most important part of the effectiveness of teaching and learning: the emotional environment.

CHAPTER 4

The emotional environment

This chapter explores the emotional environment of the classroom, what it means and its importance.

How pupils perceive your behaviour is effectively their reality – they believe what they see and feel and, much of the time, pupils' perception is very accurate. Children are hugely perceptive and intuitive when they meet adults. This is why we always involve pupils in staff interviews and often our front runners have not been offered the job owing to the feedback we receive from pupils. The responsibility we have to provide an emotionally secure, safe and caring environment should never be underestimated. The three-stage lesson observation programme was inspired by my desire to address issues with the emotional environment in the classroom.

Schools are generally good at cultivating the necessary social, emotional and ethical skills including embracing mindfulness, but do we have compassion in the classroom? (Jazaieri 2018). There is extensive research linking positive relationships to academic achievement, including teachers' engagement, clear expectations, parity and fairness, enthusiasm and affection (Stephens 2015, Connor 2016, Corradino and Fogarty 2016).

I doubt any one of us doesn't remember how particular teachers made us feel. Over the years I have seen teachers talk and act disrespectfully towards their pupils and then wonder why they have behaviour management issues in the classroom. We bring up children to challenge what is wrong, to be strong, resilient and articulate, and then expect them to be quiet when there is an injustice. Respect is mutual.

Everyone can succeed

How many times have we heard pupils say, 'I can't do that because I've been told I'm no good.' This might be a comment from home or on school. A contentious subject, but by setting and streaming pupils are we sending the wrong emotional messages? By restricting pupil activity because it doesn't fall into one our traditional moulds, are we seriously capping the potential our pupils? How many of us reading this book have rebelled and proved a point when we have been told we can't do something?

If a school's emotional environment is secure and positive, pupils will feel more confident to take risks and reach for the sky.

High-performance learning

Deborah Eyre's work on high-performance learning is captivating and challenging, in that all children should be able to achieve. Her book, *High Performance Learning: How to Become a World Class School* (2016), describes twenty advanced cognitive performance characteristics (ACPs) and ten values, attitudes and attributes (VAAs), a combination of which can be used to form a school's vision and ethos. Although values-based education is a relatively established method used across schools already, it is the ACPs that I find most exciting.

> **Deborah gives an example of a preschool child walking with her mother. She breaks away and runs into a puddle with her canvas shoes. Rather than reprimand her, she says to her daughter, 'Wiggle your toes and tell me how that feels.'**
>
> Although I don't condone blatant defiance, when are parents controlling unnecessarily? How many times have we heard parents screeching at the children in shopping centres? How many children would have been reprimanded for jumping in the puddle? This example teaches the child far more about what happens if you jump in a puddle than an explained reprimand or, worse still – and as we have all seen – more physical interaction. Learnt behaviour has a significant impact on present and future behaviours, enabling a toxic cycle of bad behaviour.

To develop such cognitive behaviours, children need to feel confident in those that care for them and be given the space to take risks without fear of redress. As with epigenetic changes to DNA through our lifetime (Johns

Hopkins Medical Institutions 2008), where inherited markers on a DNA sequence can change, influenced by diet and environmental exposure, the brain is malleable and malleability of intelligence can increase or decrease over time due to factors not only including predetermined genetics but also behaviour and external environmental conditions. A counter-argument offered by Robert Plomin in *Blueprint* (2019) suggests that you are what you are born with, illustrated through the story of identical twins and triplets. Either way, providing a safe, caring and mentally stable environment for learning is key to success. What both arguments agree on, and there will always be conflicting theses, is that the environment in which a child is raised has a significant impact on how they develop as children, into adulthood and throughout life. Therefore, lesson observation should go beyond the pedagogy, beyond the tick-box exercise, and directly into the emotional environment within the classroom. When I step into a classroom, I can sense the atmosphere; pupils' body language and responses in class speak volumes. I always put myself in the place of their mother observing 'my child': is this how I want my child to feel, being in front of this adult who has the ability to shape and nurture my child?

The responsibility is even greater if the child is not living in a positive emotional environment at home; and emotional abuse, as we know from our safeguarding training, is destructive and has far reaching consequences throughout life.

Tales of being failed

Ian Gilbert's book *The Working Class* (2018) opens with 'Letter to a teacher':

Dear Miss

You won't remember me or my name. You have failed so many of us.

On the other hand I have often had thoughts about you, and the other teachers, and about that institution which you call 'school' and about the boys that you fail.

You fail us right out into the fields and the factories and there you forget us.

Although this is an opening statement in a book about working class people, the failings of teachers and schools now and in the past are not segregated to the working class and the poor – children across all sectors are being failed by teacher behaviour.

The behaviour of teachers and how they make pupils feel was the biggest motivator for me when developing the three-stage lesson observation programme. I want children to be able to look back at their school days and recall more than one teacher who showed kindness and care, and made them feel safe to learn and progress. If pupils sense that a teacher doesn't like them for whatever reason, this is so destructive and we need to be the adult and treat all children fairly with the same opportunities and respect. This is quite poignant: because GCSE and A-level exams did not take place in 2020 owing to the COVID-19 pandemic, centres provided grades to the exam boards for statistical standardisation. The most talked about issue with regards to this is unconscious bias. Why? Because unconscious bias is in us all whether we like it or not. So much so, this is becoming a recognised trait and issue. Unconscious bias training is now statutory for teachers, management and governors of schools. Most professionals address this to ensure it does not affect their pupils, but I am sure during your career you will have seen how a member of staff acts and wondered why they are teaching, as it is apparent they don't like children.

How many teachers are so miserable in their own lives that this control and misery follows them into school? Those who are genuine and work with passion and care have nothing to fear from the focus on emotional environment, whereas the superficial and insincere are exposed by the three-stage lesson observation programme. During the observation, and from your own encounters with the member of staff, you know if the emotions of the children in the class are safe with this teacher.

By challenging staff behaviour and attitudes, we have sent a very strong message that bad tempers, moods or irrational and bullying behaviour will not be tolerated. This is written clearly within our code of conduct. If you are a headteacher and in your heart you know this is happening in your school, be brave and deal with it. If you are one of these teachers – leave the profession!

Lesson observation gives us all the opportunity to learn through a collaborative approach, opening discussion and dialogue, and even the opportunity for more direct and honest conversations. All teachers can be quietly brilliant within the confines of their own personalities through a nurturing, coaching environment – no one expects a staffroom of charismatic adventurers! A good balance of styles and personalities is conducive to a good learning environment for pupils.

What does good or even excellent look like? There is no right or wrong methodology or theoretical practice in the classroom (Zaare 2013). There is no one-size-fits-all and observers should embrace individuality – after all, if it works: brilliant! We know the charismatic, courageous classroom adventurers: the teachers with colourful tales, intellectual sparkle, humour (often bordering on the side of reckless!), those with the loudest cheers in assemblies or prize-giving – known as 'the legend'. We know the unassuming, quiet deliverer of brilliance, widely respected, balanced and diligent. But we also know the passive deliverer of mediocrity – and this is not good enough for our children.

I asked a former pupil whom I taught in the late 1990s about his experiences in school. Iain Bell, now one of the 21st century's most prolific and successful composers, embraced school and those who taught him. Iain has shown resilience and determination to succeed, and the fact that he has kept in touch with his teachers and honoured them in his operas' programmes is testament to the memories he has of those positive teachers who believed the sky and beyond was reachable.

I have included his thoughts within the book as his feelings about school, his memories of how he was made to feel, are still very much with him.

When you were at school, what were the qualities of excellent teachers for you?

Beyond a mastery of their subject matter, to have a teacher so enthused by their topic that they could passionately expound for minutes on end on one tiny facet was an inspiration. This would afford a glimpse into their own private joys and areas of interest that would usually remain hidden, but on the occasions it was revealed would never fail to inspire. Passion is always infectious.

During the later years of secondary education (around Years 11–13), I felt particular teachers beginning to respond to classes and, more importantly, to individuals on a more adult level to which I responded very positively. This could be the conferring of respect and trust in me to carry out a particular duty of seemingly high responsibility (in my case, the tuition of a younger student struggling with their French studies, or being asked to play the piano for a school musical), or something ostensibly small yet deeply affecting, like the sharing of a joke between the teacher and me, or the warm and friendly running jokes built up organically between the class and teacher.

iere a particular moment at school when a teacher made you ally proud, gave you confidence or inspiration? How do you feel about that now?

Making a living as a classical musician, it was the music department to which I clung the tightest during my secondary school years, the respect deepening, hopefully on both sides, as my studies progressed. These student–teacher relationships without a doubt instilled the confidence in me with which I was able to forge a career as a professional musician. These important moments were not those in which I learned a specific detail or fact, but rather occasions where the teacher took the time to praise me for my efforts, with sincerity. Music is something in which you have to constantly strive in multiple disciplines in order to improve, whether that's your instrumental playing, your grasp of counterpoint or knowledge of the repertoire, so to have that reflected back meant a great deal indeed. I recall one particular Music History A-level mock exam paper being returned to me, marked, saying 88% 'This is excellent'. The 88% was obviously lovely to read, but the fact the teacher took the time to qualify it meant the world to me, allowing me to know that excellence could be in my grasp. Another music teacher page-turned for me whilst I played the harpsichord in an orchestral performance of a Vivaldi work, and I recall her saying 'You played that really well this evening'. She didn't need to say anything, so the fact she said that meant the world to me.

Did a teacher ever make you feel bad about yourself? How do you feel about that now?

In Year 8, we studied the Tudors, a historic period with which I had long had a great affinity, even taking it upon myself in primary school to learn the dates of the monarchs' reigns and other similar details. This enthusiasm poured into the classroom and there was one particular lesson in which I had been inspired to 'put my hand up' to answer several questions. After a couple of correct answers, I recall the teacher bristling, pointedly saying something on the lines of (and I paraphrase) 'Yes, we know *you* know'. I recall feeling a little embarrassed and angry that my own independent hard work was being devalued. It didn't stop me from pursuing my own independent studies, though. This is the first time I've given that moment any real thought, and though it is clear the teacher in question could have handled the situation better, it must have been frustrating having a class full of pupils who were mildly uninterested, with just the one actively participating.

Can you remember a lesson that was observed by another member of staff? If so, did the behaviour of the teacher change?

Almost. I recall our school being inspected by Ofsted in the mid 1990s, and in one GCSE class our teacher, who was a very experienced, gifted teacher, regularly glancing over to the door to see if the inspectors were waiting outside, preparing to make their way in to observe. I recall feeling sorry for her; seeing someone so confident and together needlessly feeling personally scrutinised was upsetting. The inspectors did indeed come to observe the class, and whilst she maintained her high standards of information delivery and inclusion, the personality and sparkle had temporarily vanished.

If you could give three pieces of advice to a teacher, what would they be?

- Don't ever self-censor your personality. As students, we respond to strong personalities at a time we ourselves are on the path to forging our own. We need and crave our role models to show us differing ways of being, so be *you*. I always responded most deeply to the teachers who had the strongest, even most eccentric personalities, whether that was expressed in an out-there dress sense, unusual speaking voice or distinctive manner.
- Affirmation, for me, was the key to my confidence. The littlest words can go so far, even if the pupil doesn't show it externally.
- Don't always give the class clown the lead role in the play. Though they may be funny, gregarious and confident in the classroom, and it can be a channel for their energies, they are often a bully in the playground, and this only serves to validate their behaviour.

Emotional environment for teachers

Iain's response to the question about lesson observation is, unfortunately, the experience of many teachers, and I had a similar physical experience (described in the Introduction) when Ofsted inspected my first school.

...otional environment in the classroom and in school is equally ...t for a teacher. It is terrible that Iain's recollection of the teachers' ....ing observed has stayed with him; no teacher should be made to feel like this.

Showing positivity and a secure emotional environment catches on, and – I know this sounds a little superficial – yawning or giggling when you are not supposed to happens because it's infectious! If we show kindness, care and consideration, we will get it back from the children. When we see a child's eyes light up, don't ours too? And in return our emotional well-being improves.

Creating a positive emotional environment builds trust in the class, not just between pupils and teachers but also teachers and leaders. If we all share the same vision and understand the challenges it brings, we are all in it together.

What does an emotionally healthy classroom look like?

An emotionally healthy classroom will be where a pupil wants to be. They might not be the best at the subject, or have a belief they are no good, but they should feel they are safe to express themselves, take risks with learning and contribute to the class for positive collaborative learning. Each child should feel that the teacher is reaching them individually. This is a tough call for teachers but with the good resources we have and the more effective use of technology, including blended learning, it is achievable.

The room should feel friendly, including displays. Clear expectations of behaviour and classroom code are key. Collaborative learning and active pupil engagement will be prevalent and there will be time to go off-piste, time to reflect, time to inspire next steps and promote independent learning. All this is achievable through trust.

What does an emotionally healthy school look like?

There always has to be someone at the top making final decisions, but an emotionally healthy school doesn't rely on hierarchy to breathe positivity, create a vibrant learning environment and make the school a happy place to be. It has to be a culture, and the leader's role is to lead by example and give a clear vision and direction as to what the emotionally healthy school looks like. Being a school leader isn't easy and those schools that are part of an umbrella organisation will have the continuing task of managing above and below to promote the importance of an emotionally healthy environment, especially to those where the bottom line is the key indicator of success.

Direct communication and transparency are key for the psychological contract with staff and part of that contract is providing an emotionally secure environment. It doesn't mean life is all good – that's misguided. Take 2020, for instance, and the impact of the COVID-19 pandemic on all schools. Independent schools have had to make tough financial decisions that have resulted in redundancies. My advice is not to hide the discomfort and impending pain but to be honest about why the school or organisation is making these decisions. Promote the good times and embrace the bad times so that staff understand and can themselves plan ahead. In an emotionally healthy school, any problems can be overcome collaboratively working together.

Underhand communication is insidious and one thing I can't abide is bcc'd emails. Good for blanket information to protect confidentiality but in other instances it's malicious and unnecessary. Gossip beyond naturally tame speculation is harmful and I would advise it is described in staff contracts and code of conduct documents as being seen as undermining the school or organisation and can be a disciplinary offence. Set out your stall – if you show transparency, honesty and clarity in thought, vision and communication, these too are infectious and your psychological contract with staff will be such that a collective and shared vision is prevalent throughout the school.

The three-stage lesson observation programme supports this culture. I often have staff invite me to classes or say, 'If you're passing, come on in and see this.' They want people in the classroom to share what they are doing, and do not fear being watched. Stage 3 of the programme is also a fabulous opportunity to share one-to-one time with a member of staff to coach and mentor them. Underlying issues often emerge and even though you probably can't help, lending a listening ear is a great relief and solace for a member of staff. To be able to share is conducive to a safe, secure and positive emotional environment.

How you make people feel will set a benchmark for the way others will make one another feel. How you make someone feel is key to success. We should all feel that we can reach beyond the sky.

Awe and wonder

An emotionally secure and healthy environment will breathe awe and wonder. We are all capable of creating awe and wonder; it's just having the confidence to go ahead and do it. What does awe and wonder look like?

When I observe a class, I want to see the awe and wonder where learning and space and time are given to children to explore concepts and they're encouraged to think. Awe and wonder can be found in just the topic that is being shared, such as black holes or discovering mathematical equations relating to dimensions, but all topics and subjects can be communicated in such a way.

Recently, I observed a Year 6 lesson on 'the meaning of life', where quite amazing ideas flowed freely in a supportive and respectful environment. It truly was an amazing moment and I know these children will look back fondly on their fabulous teacher. The atmosphere in this class was almost electric – one of those moments that lifts you out of everyday experiences and where the human mind is truly explored. The learning journey and experience for the children I encountered in that observation hasn't left me.

Our Head of Maths firmly believes in learning through problem-solving. She invited me to her class and when I entered you could have heard a pin drop until a pupil squealed 'I've got it!' – a true Eureka! moment. The ruckus that ensued was not disturbance but the eagerness of other pupils to share the solution and the journey to the solution. They were mesmerised – it could have been snowing in summer outside and they wouldn't have noticed.

There are many examples and they are not just cerebral. During a Stage 3 discussion with a history teacher, she told me of an event in her class that, again, was awesome. One Year 7 pupil was struggling with organisation and the teacher gave her a large paper clip to help collate her worksheets. The next lesson, the young girl still had the paper clip, but it was dressed as a person and had become her organisation partner. The other children in the class wanted paper clips too, and within days they all had organisation partners in the form of dressed paper clips. Of course, there were moments when the organisation buddies had to be put away in blazer pockets so as not to be too much of a fashion contest, but they served a purpose – and boy, was that class organised. Their creativity and collaboration created a wonderfully supportive emotional environment with clear boundaries. They won't forget this – nor will I.

In conclusion

Imagine walking around your school and experiencing one class after another creating this awe and wonder, which in turn creates this wonderfully healthy and happy and positive emotional environment. To see light in the eyes of teachers and pupils burn brightly as they interact with enthusiasm and mutual respect. To feel the electric environment of positivity, the genuine desire to learn – and an inspirational learning environment is all we want, as leaders, for our children.

Part 2

The three-stage model
An overview

This chapter takes a general overview of the three-stage lesson observation programme, the roles and responsibilities of those involved, what its objectives are and how it is set up. Can it be successful in all schools?

The three stages

Stage 1: The observation

An observation where the primary focus is the emotional environment in the classroom. This can be planned or unannounced by heads of department (HoDs) or the senior management team (SMT). Paperwork is sent through to SMT undertaking Stage 2.

Stage 2: The nuts and bolts

A meeting with a member of SMT to talk through all other aspects of a teacher's role outside the classroom, including planning, marking, report writing and work scrutiny. Paperwork from Stages 1 and 2 is sent to the headteacher for Stage 3.

Stage 3: Meeting with the headteacher

A final meeting to discuss Stages 1 and 2, management competencies where applicable, and contribution to wider school life; that is, co-curricular contribution, tutoring and whole-school projects.

All paperwork mentioned is given in the next three chapters for each stage.

Responsibility of the headteacher

Headteachers have the responsibility to ensure that practices are fair and the quality of teaching is good, if not excellent, at all times. There will be times when problems arise for one reason or another and this may then initiate a more formal process. It would need to be a disaster for me to take this measure as I believe we will all have times when we fail for various reasons. The programme gives an opportunity to nurture and bring forward teachers in a positive forum away from formal procedures with the collaboration and cooperation of other staff if appropriate.

I believe that my experiences of being wounded as a child in the education system have made me particularly empathetic to those who have also been wounded, whether child or adult. Often, an application form will be glowing with an impressive work record and qualifications, only for you to discover that the person sitting in front of you is possibly a shadow of their former self. Although this is never raised in an interview, an intuitive head will see when the candidate has diminished over time in their workplace. Headteachers must ensure this doesn't happen and the health and well-being of staff should be taken seriously. This also applies to bullying in the workplace which, unfortunately, is still apparent across many industries. Staff should be given a good chance to succeed with autonomy and the tools to do the job. Job descriptions should be tight so a blame culture cannot exist and accountability at all levels prevails. All staff should have the confidence to put their hands up when something goes wrong and then work together to put it right. Again, a brave head will spot talent and nurture it even if it has seemingly lost its sparkle along the way.

The zebra at the back of the pack

All schools have a zebra at the back of the pack, a lion nipping at its tail. When the back runner gets taken out, it is always replaced with another and this is a costly recruitment exercise for all schools. It is the head's responsibility to ensure that the zebra at the back of the pack is given the tools to succeed through coaching and mentoring, because once running with the pack, its collective strength will be felt by the whole school. If a teacher fails, whose fault is it? It is not solely the fault of the teacher but a collective responsibility from the head downwards.

The three-stage lesson observation programme allows many opportunities to help teachers progress no matter what level they are at. Ultimately, the happiness of staff will rub off on the pupils and it doesn't take long for this happiness to uplift the whole school.

It's important to remember too that teachers tend to be promoted because of their excellence in the classroom and not their abilities as managers. Discussing management competencies during Stage 3 also opens a good discussion on what training or support a member of staff needs, and also gives a good idea on succession planning for the future.

The three-stage lesson observation programme was born out of the desire to see the emotional environment in the classroom flourish and, therefore, as head and leader, if this is your mission too, it needs to be communicated with conviction to the team and staff as a whole. You may feel that the emotional environment within the school is already excellent and there is a greater need to focus on Stage 1 observations.

Does it involve everyone?

Yes. All teaching staff are involved across our school from Reception to Year 13. The only differences are the pupil feedback forms from Year 3, which are straightforward and geared towards levels of happiness. There are no feedback forms for the children below Year 3 for obvious reasons.

In a school of our size (over 800 pupils) the aim is to complete one whole cycle of Stages 1, 2 and 3 by the start of March. HoDs' observations, learning walks and work scrutiny are additional practices that occur throughout the week.

From a logistical point of view, once members of the senior management team have agreed who does what, a member of the administrative team can set up the lesson observation and meetings in advance with the recommended length of time between each stage. This is clearly laid out in the suggested teaching and learning policy below.

It is essential to be organised and not cancel observations or meetings. In a busy school it would be so easy to do so, but this will cause delays in the process and hinder progress. This is especially true in the early years of the programme when its credibility is still in its infancy.

What about 'Titan' schools?

In the UK there are many schools with over 1,000 pupils; some have in excess of 2,500, with up to 12 academic staff on their senior management team.

LVS Ascot had 850 pupils in the first year of the three-stage lesson observation programme. Bearing in mind that the average class size in the school is 15 pupils, chances are the school has the same amount of academic staff as a state school with a school roll of 1,700 pupils. The SMT at LVS Ascot comprised six members, although one of those was dedicated to running the infant and junior school. Therefore, looking at the pupil numbers and size of SMT at each of the 'Titan' schools mentioned above, the raw physical logistics of carrying out the programme is possible. There is a very good local state school close to LVS Ascot that runs almost two separate schools with a dual timetable and two headteachers, and another school that is divided into four separate houses, each managed separately with its own dedicated staff. In larger schools, the organisation and structure would be key to having the staffing resources to implement the three-stage lesson observation programme.

However, there are a number of concerns or barriers to the successful implementation of the programme.

1) Some of the 'Titan' schools, have been forced to increase their pupil roll number beyond what would be classed as reasonable – in fact, reckless – by the LEA. Without the physical resources and staffing capacity, no wonder many of them are in special measures.

2) Some schools are highly unionised and headteachers will need an appetite for a challenge to implement the programme. It could be that the head does not believe in lesson observation or, as my survey revealed, has 'bigger fish to fry'.

3) Some schools have demanding behavioural issues. I visited a school in east London where the head showing me around the school was consciously aware of the fact that there could be a lockdown at any time.

4) Pupil feedback in more challenging schools where behaviour is a key issue could be a non-starter and not statistically viable, if possible at all. Staff will be under enough pressure as it is without the fear of retribution through the questionnaires.

5) Schools have bigger issues to worry about, such as monetary resources and also child poverty, with many children coming to school without a meal or uniform. Some schools now have their own food banks. Without such fundamental basics, lesson observation would be very far down the list of priorities.

6) In Chapter 4's discussion of attitudes towards lesson observation, it is very clear that there is a negative mindset with underlying fear and no appetite in many schools to embrace this change.

I believe, though, that despite the pressures above, if a head really believes this could work in their school, it will work. Even if the programme was watered down to:

a) Stage 1: A five-minute observation as part of a learning walk.
b) Stage 2: A meeting with a senior manager or HoD regarding factors outside the classroom.
c) Stage 3: A meeting with the head. Heads, no matter how busy, should ensure this happens in their school. The support it shows, and the building of the psychological contract will make staff feel appreciated and supported within a demanding school and a very demanding job. More than anything, to retain staff will be a big challenge and this is one way to do it.

Going back to my first headteacher, he didn't have time for scheduled meetings but would join us on duty for ten minutes, or over lunch to build relationships and reflect on our work. Staff value individual attention from their head, so in response I'd open that closed door, manage my diary effectively and set time aside for the greatest asset a school has for success: its staff.

Maybe the three-stage lesson observation programme is a complete nonstarter for you and your school. The day-to-day logistics, demands and restrictions you face might make this purely a pipe dream. But with the right conviction and vision, it can be done, even though it may take more time and be a little more painful and frustrating, chipping away gradually at the barriers.

Our journey

In our first year, HoDs undertook planned observations owing to the nature of the school culture, which was quite hostile and unionised. This is not to say unions are bad, because they safeguard us all from unscrupulous practice, but the common room had an anti-management culture and union guidelines were always used as an attack rather than negotiation, stopping the school moving forward. There might always be one or two antagonists fighting change just for the sake of it, and if they are influential, this can be troublesome in implementing change.

It was surprising that when staff were presented with the idea of the threestage lesson observation programme (the antagonists having moved on), there appeared to be little or no resistance, although there were some very well-structured theoretical debates regarding Stage 1 and the lack of peda-gogical content and focus. This challenge came from staff who were very keen on teaching and learning with experience elsewhere, and obviously this approach collided slightly or more than slightly with their experiences and expectations of lesson observation. These staff were not objectors, just really passionate about teaching and learning, and found it hard to disentangle their embedded beliefs to realise that observation outcomes don't always have to rely on tangible factual pedagogy but basic gut feeling about what is happening in the classroom. We overcame this with discussions, taking time to listen to those staff, and gently challenging them to step outside of their comfort zones.

It is difficult sometimes to bring across the message that we don't have to do things the way others do or the way current theory and practice dictates. This is what made the three-stage lesson observation so refreshing and chal-lenging in itself.

The cultural shift towards to the emotional environment took time as there was a level of suspicion that the focus could be so simple as human inter-action and there were no ulterior motives, especially as the process was not used as part of formal appraisal and performance management. I can under-stand that some staff, especially those early in their careers, may still feel uncomfortable in their default persona in the classroom and how this might be judged. As we gain more experience, we do become more comfortable with who we are, we accept who we are and expect others to accept us too. I wanted staff to be comfortable in their own skins in a safe environment and take away the stress and anxiety of having to perform. It's like in an inter-view when the candidate is ticking the boxes with all the right answers and you're looking in their eyes thinking, 'Hey, come on. There's so much more to you!' Ask them about something they are expert at or passionate about and see how individuals relax, become animated and excited, technical lan-guage flows, stories emerge and inspiration fills the room. If you can capture this, bottle it and then use it 24/7 in a school, your pupils will be inspired and in awe at what learning offers.

What I find after six years of the process is that the level of risk-taking in the classroom has increased and the awe and wonder in classes is tremen-dous. Although objectives and learning have to take priority, often in very pressurised environments where results are the bottom line, it is excellent to see time taken to go off-piste, explore surrounding topics and listen to the views and ideas of others – often electric atmospheres, places of real aca-demic and philosophical debate: a place to really learn.

Although this book presents data and statistics to measure its success, it's not about numbers in the classroom, nor tick-box exercises as with standard, mundane lesson observation forms. It's about gut feeling, intuition and the atmosphere in the classroom.

Bringing people with you

As mentioned previously, I had always felt that HoDs were being too kind to their department colleagues; but not wanting to disenfranchise them and needing them to be part of the journey, the Stage 1 observation was carried out by them in the first year. They arranged planned observations with their teams and the HoDs then observed each other. To gauge the accuracy of the HoDs' perceptions of what was happening in the class, pupil feedback was introduced to correspond directly with what the lesson observation focused on.

Later in the book, I give more detail about how we set up the three-stage lesson observation programme. The implementation journey started with a staff meeting to present the vision, held before the end of the academic year; this was to put it into the minds of staff that lesson observation would change from the start of the new academic year. We took up the debates and theoretical challenges from staff as above and ensured that HoD meetings clearly presented the objectives and desired outcomes to ensure consistency across the school. Policies were updated ahead of the new academic year, and discussed and talked through in presentations and meetings.

The pupil feedback forms are an essential part of the process; they are almost like a control in a science experiment. Children are so hugely intuitive and perceptive, and they do not mince their words if they feel aggrieved. I trust their judgement to be fair and it is very easy to see by analysing their responses across the school where particular issues might be. I thought if there would be any kickback, it would have been with the pupil feedback forms, as this is quite intrusive for staff, but we experienced very little resistance and angst at all.

Essential to the understanding and credibility of the three-stage lesson observation programme is a teaching and learning policy that 'breathes' the vision and articulates expectations. Everyone in the process needs to understand what their role in the process is, so including the roles and responsibilities within the policy sets out those expectations.

The teaching and learning policy template

Principles, intent and aims

Aside from safeguarding and related policies, the teaching and learning policy at [school] is the most important policy the school has. [School] recognises that our purpose is to provide our pupils with the best possible learning experience. Every lesson is precious and time lost through not providing the best first time, every time cannot be reclaimed. Our teaching and learning policy reflects current academic theory and practice, the focus of ISI and Ofsted frameworks and provides a tool for us to meet the needs of every child.

We believe that all children have the ability to succeed and reach beyond expectation. Our teaching and support staff are the facilitators of excellent practice, which enables all children to fulfil their expectations and aspirations. We believe that children have a significant voice in their teaching and learning, and consultation with pupils during the lesson observation process is key to our understanding of the service we provide.

Our primary focus is one of happiness – an emotional environment of mutual respect and understanding to ensure the classroom is conducive to effective learning and optimum productivity.

Therefore, our teaching and learning aims are to:

- Provide a positive emotional environment in the classroom, in activities and in recreational time.
- Create a positive, happy, supportive and mutually respectful community.
- Provide the best: first time, every time.
- Expect the best: first time, every time.
- Possess and deliver excellent subject knowledge.
- Deliver clearly our knowledge and challenge misunderstanding.
- Challenge all pupils to achieve of their best.

The principles, intent and aims of this policy apply to all children at [school], although we recognise the specific aspects amended for younger children.

Our responsibilities as teachers

The emotional environment

- To ensure that lessons begin on time and a register is taken.
- To ensure that behaviour in the classroom, in activities and during recreational time is exemplary.
- To create a positive, welcoming and friendly environment in the classroom.
- To encourage positive communication and praise.
- To foster a culture of positive eye contact, active presence and participation in the classroom.
- To ensure the classroom is safe, calm, orderly, and free from ridicule.
- To foster an environment of mutual respect and understanding with a commitment to learning.
- Encourage pupils to be aspirational in their learning, ideas and activities.

The nuts and bolts

- To ensure lesson objectives are clearly stated and understood by all.
- To ensure lessons are progressive in line with the scheme of work and that prior knowledge is evidenced through rigorous questioning and challenge.
- To ensure that the pace and content of the lesson challenges all pupils.
- To ensure that pupils' learning is enhanced by clear engagement and active participation.
- To ensure subject knowledge is excellent and clearly communicated, with any misunderstandings or inaccuracies are challenged.
- To ensure lessons are fully inclusive and differentiated allowing all pupils to progress.
- To deliver varied tasks and activities with opportunities for speaking, listening and writing.
- To ensure key concepts are taught for long-term memory in context rather than as isolated, disjointed facts.

Independence

- To encourage pupils to set their own success criteria to allow progress.
- To provide opportunities for self-assessment to allow for reflection and progression.
- To encourage collaborative learning to enhance attitudes to learning.
- To provide opportunities for independent learning in the classroom, in activities and outdoor play.

Technical

- Provide opportunities for the use of ICT where appropriate.
- Provide numeracy challenges within the lesson.
- Encourage pupils to read and sing where appropriate.
- Select varied resources to enhance practical activities.
- Challenge literacy issues.
- Ensure assessment and marking reflects department and whole-school policies.
- Planning is progressive.
- Report writing is accurate, on time and informs progress.

British values/spiritual, moral, social and cultural development (SMSC)

- Ensure schemes of work and lesson plans identify key aspects of British values.
- Provide opportunities to embrace the key aspects of British values.
- Encourage debate.
- Promote inclusivity and embrace diversity.
- Encourage and foster community spirit and support in all we do.

The wow factor

- To be different: create a little awe and wonder.
- To ensure pupils are motivated by challenge and inspiration.
- To challenge myself in my teaching.
- Ensure pupils are engaged by exciting and imaginative lessons.

- Encourage pupils to be aspirational.
- Encourage pupils to take risks with their learning.

Effectiveness of our teaching and learning is evidenced through:

- Our bespoke three-stage lesson observation programme.
- Head of department and peer observations.
- Work scrutiny.
- Learning walks.

Responsibilities of heads of department

- To draw up a departmental observation plan for the heads of department and peer observation within the department.
- Report back to the academic performance leader any matters arising from the observations.
- Discuss the observations and general matters arising at department meetings.
- Provide support, training and guidance to staff to achieve maximum potential.
- Lead by example.

Responsibilities of senior management

- Be objective and impartial during lesson observations.
- Provide constructive feedback and recognise good practice.
- Be empathetic.
- Offer advice, coaching and support where appropriate.

Responsibilities of governors

- Ensure this policy is adhered to.
- Ensure consistent, fair and effective implementation of this policy.
- Question and challenge the senior management on the lesson observation process and its findings.
- To observe senior management during the process where appropriate.
- To report back to the full governing body on the effectiveness of the programme.

All staff should expect one round of the three-stage lesson observation programme per academic year, although new staff may have two rounds. All staff will take part in department/peer observations, work scrutiny and learning walks. The whole observation programme is not designed to be onerous or intrusive but a celebration of the excellent practice throughout the school and the opportunities to learn with our peers.

The three-stage lesson observation programme

The programme was designed to provide a consistent and unbiased approach to lesson observation which is separate from formal appraisal, centring on the outcomes for pupils, and to celebrate and share good practice across the school. [School] recognises that lesson observation can be subjective and should not rely on the opinion of one person but a collective and collaborative approach to achieve a holistic view of the quality of teaching and learning across the school. [School] also recognises that as the focus of national teaching changes over time, including the inspection framework, we also respond to the changing needs of our own school and, therefore, the lesson observation programme will be adapted and amended accordingly.

The underlying purpose of the Stage 1 observation is to gauge the emotional environment in the classroom and across the school, which has been proven to enhance learning in a safe, happy environment where good practice and excellent teaching is celebrated.

All relevant forms for all Stages are available on the network.

Stage 1

The Stage 1 lesson observation will be unannounced and undertaken by the headteacher. The focus of the inspection will be in line with the areas of responsibility above. Workbooks or examples of work will be taken at the end of the lesson and returned to reception within 24 hours. A pupil feedback questionnaire will be collected at the end of the lesson.

Stage 2

The Stage 2 meeting will be held with another member of the senior management team within five working days of Stage 1. During Stage 2, discussion will take place on marking and assessment, planning and the standard of report writing.

Stage 3

The Stage 3 meeting will be held with the headteacher within five working days of Stage 2 and will focus on feedback from stages 1 and 2, as well as evaluation of co-curricular contribution and management competencies where appropriate.

Head of department and peer observation programme

The academic performance leader will work with heads of department to ensure there is a comprehensive and rigorous programme of peer observations within the department and outside the department. This is separate and independent of the three-stage lesson observation programme. Lesson observations should appear as an agenda item on department minutes to discuss sharing good practice and any matters arising.

Work scrutiny

As well as work samples being taken as part of Stage 1, heads of department will take regular audits of department workbooks to assure quality and assess consistency across the department. At various points throughout the academic year, the academic performance leader and headteacher undertake random checks across year groups and different groups such as SEN, and boarding and day pupils.

Workbooks should:

- Be kept clean and tidy, and covered where appropriate.
- Contain all department marking and assessment criteria including grading ladders within the front and back covers.
- Be marked regularly in line with department and whole-school marking policies.
- Give formative and summative feedback where appropriate, informing where progress can be made.
- Show evidence of missed or not good enough work being passed back to be done again.
- Secure all loose sheets.

Learning walks

Learning walks are invaluable to experience the flavour of what is happening in school at a particular time of the day. Learning walks are organised in advance by the academic performance leader who will invite all staff through the shared calendar to join him on a walk. The focus of each walk will be published with the date. Topics in previous years have included the use of humour and the power of silence.

Reviewed: [Date]
To be reviewed no later than: [Date]
Author: [Name, role]

- **During COVID-19 restrictions, lesson observations continue as set out in this policy, but a degree of flexibility and the challenges of blended, flipped and remote learning are taken into consideration. More than ever, the emotional environment of lessons is paramount to happiness and success.**

In conclusion

Set out your stall formally in a written process backed by a clear and concise policy so that staff can see this is a formal school process. In other words, it's going to happen: embrace it!

CHAPTER 6

Stage 1
The observation itself

This chapter describes Stage 1 of the three-stage lesson observation pro-gramme: its objectives; how it can be implemented according to what your school wants to achieve; how it may be changed and adapted over time; your role in the programme; and the expectations of others.

Objectives of Stage 1

The objectives of the Stage 1 observation are to remove the old baggage of previous traditional lesson observations, to take away the fear and the link to formal appraisal and performance management. It is only too clear that pupils do not benefit from their teachers being part of planned observa-tion; the lesson will not be typical and will result in a false snapshot of pupil experience with this teacher.

However, where the school is culturally will depend on how Stage 1 observations are undertaken in the first year. It is important to bring staff with you and heads should assess the risks of how they proceed in the first year, even if it takes two to three years to get to the unannounced observa-tion. It could be that Stage 1 observations in the first year are announced and with good notice, such as five working days, and a preliminary meeting held before the observation to affirm and reassure the teacher of the objectives. Gradually – and heads will gauge the temperature of feeling in the common room as trust builds – Stage 1 can move to unannounced observations and this could be sooner rather than later for many schools. You don't want to cause damage, and staff may see a sudden change as being superficially thought through and fail to bring them on the journey.

If the culture of the school is negative, suspicious of management and its practices, as well as being fearful of observation, planned observations by the head of department in the first year under this more formal structure is a soft approach. It will not have the desired effect of moving away from planned lessons or inconsistency across departments, but staff will have the discomfort of Stages 2 and 3 in the first year with senior management, which may be enough change in the first year.

It might be the culture of the school is stable enough for middle-of-the-road change by bringing all the observations under one member of the SMT but still with notice of Stage 1 observations.

Brave heads who want radical change or those schools that benefit from an excellent, trusting and supportive culture may jump straight in with a complete overhaul of their lesson observation programme. This would entail moving straight into unannounced lesson observations under the SMT and, ideally for consistency, by the same member of the team.

You need to be clear about what you hope to achieve from the lesson observation and have clear outcomes in mind. This may come from previous data the school has collected, and feedback from staff, pupils and parents. Data gathering is essential to give the focus of the lesson observation a purpose.

The cultural shift in the lesson observation is away from pedagogical content and towards a focus on the emotional environment of the classroom. This may take time, hence caution in radical change. Once the focus starts to shift, it is easier to remove the HoD from the process and guide them towards department observations where pedagogy and specific learning outcomes can be scrutinised more thoroughly with department members to share good practice.

What did the first year bring?

In the first year, to test our assumptions of HoDs being too kind in their observations, the following questions were asked of the HoD and pupils, and rated on Likert scale responses.

Classroom observation survey (in 2014 undertaken by HoDs)

Table 6.1 Classroom observation survey

Emotional Environment (EM)	Strongly Agree	Agree	Disagree	Strongly Disagree
There is a warm welcome to the class				
The teacher is active in the classroom				
There is good eye contact				
The teacher uses positive communication and praise where due				

Classroom Management (CM)	Strongly Agree	Agree	Disagree	Strongly Disagree
There are high expectations of behaviour				
The lesson begins on time				
The register is taken				
Bad behaviour is dealt with quickly and effectively				

Teaching and Learning (TL)	Strongly Agree	Agree	Disagree	Strongly Disagree
Pupils are aware of the objectives of the lesson				
Effective differentiation allows all pupils to progress				
Ideas are communicated clearly and effectively				
Teacher subject knowledge is excellent				
There is evidence of prior learning				
Teacher questioning reinforces learning				
The lesson is inclusive and stimulating				

Pupil questionnaire

Table 6.2 Pupil questionnaire

	Strongly agree	*Agree*	*Disagree*	*Strongly disagree*
The classroom is a positive place to be (EM)				
I feel I can ask for help when needed (EM)				
My teacher gives praise when due (EM)				
My teacher is enthusiastic for this subject (EM)				
I enjoy the lesson (EM)				
My classmates behave well in this lesson (CM)				
The lesson begins on time (CM)				
My teacher tackles bad behaviour effectively (CM)				
I know what I need to do to improve (TL)				
Ideas are presented clearly and effectively (TL)				
My teacher's subject knowledge is excellent (TL)				

Findings from 2014/15

Table 6.3 2014/15 findings

Subject	EM Teacher	EM Pupil	CM Teacher	CM Pupil	TL Teacher	TL Pupil	Typical Lesson
A	100%	100%	100%	75.8%	97%	72%	82.2%
B	100%	92.3%	100%	69.6%	100%	78.3%	84.4%
C	100%	89%	100%	78%	99%	86%	49.9%
D	100%	82.7%	100%	63.5%	100%	71.5%	88.6%
E	100%	74.2%	100%	83%	100%	80.7%	70.7%
F	100%	90.6%	99%	86.8%	98.7%	92.5%	91.3%
G	100%	90%	100%	70.8%	100%	86.4%	77.3%
H	100%	91.7%	100%	90.5%	100%	91.9%	90%
I	100%	92.2%	100%	91.2%	95%	90.8%	80.73%
J	94.8%	82%	90%	88.3%	72.5%	86.1%	92.2%
K	100%	83.3%	94%	75%	96.1%	52%	91.7%
L	100%	87.5%	98.8%	82.7%	96%	83.5%	82.7%
M	100%	72.8%	95.4%	80%	92.4%	79.3%	82.5%
N	95.4%	90.6%	87.3%	93.3%	85.8%	90%	80%
O	98.9%	88.9%	100%	86.6%	100%	85.3%	82.2%
Average	99.3%	87.2%	97.6%	81%	95%	81.7%	81.7%

The results weren't particularly surprising and were probably a little more positive than anticipated. The boxes highlighted in black are where there were significant differences between the HoDs' perception of what was happening in the class and the pupils' perception. As you can see, there are quite a few 100% scores in the HoDs' ratings.

What is particularly interesting and not surprising are the low scores for typicality. The amount of cells indicated in black show that, overall, pupils felt the observed lesson was not what they were used to getting. Further investigation and talking to pupils revealed that teacher behaviour and the standard of the lesson changed significantly when the lesson was being observed. No real surprises here, I hear you say. One particular subject, subject C, scored a damning 49.9% for typicality, which raised concerns about the practice within this department and prompted further investigation. The cells in grey indicate a very measured and realistic approach from the HoD, with pupil perceptions of good practice being more favourable than the HoD's perception. This was a brave and candid approach taken by the HoD, whom I remember to be a straight-talking and bright leader who went on to be vice-principal in a multi-academy trust.

As a result of the findings of year one, the rumblings of parental complaints with regards to classroom behaviour in particular, standard of teaching and marking issues, the focus of Stage 1 remained the same for the next few years, but always with the primary focus of the emotional environment being the most important.

The Stage 1 observation is not rigid and set in stone. The great thing about it is that it can be used for self-reflection and school evaluation, which will be covered in Chapter 12. From one year's findings to another, new areas of focus or need can be introduced, and staff are keen to understand what the holistic whole school message looks like.

After six years, I have taken back sole responsibility for Stage 1 observations, which gives me contact with staff and pupils, and provides me with confidence that the school is on track for continued success and that our pupils and staff are happy.

Lesson observations are now unannounced. As a busy leader, committing to get them done is a challenge. With an academic staff of over 100, aiming to finish the process by the end of the spring term takes good planning. I block out two hours at a time in my diary at various points in the week and add in the name, subject and venue. Depending on the layout of the school, it is ideal to pencil three lessons into one hour. In many formal inspection lesson observations, lesson observations are more of a learning walk. There used to be a 26-minute guideline for an observation but this appears unnecessary. Within 15 minutes, it is possible to gather all the necessary evidence, especially when the lesson ticks every box. If the lesson doesn't tick the right boxes, stay longer or, in extreme cases, inform the member of staff during Stage 3 that you will be coming back at a later time for particular reasons.

How the Stage 1 form looked in 2018/19

Table 6.4 Revised observation form 2018/19

Emotional Environment of the classroom	Yes	No	Notes
The lesson begins on time			
The register is taken			
There are high expectations of behaviour			
The teacher is aware of student activity throughout the room			
The classroom environment is positive, friendly and welcoming			
The teacher uses positive communication and praise			
The Lesson	Yes	No	Notes
Pupils are aware of the lesson's learning objective			
Pupils' learning is enhanced by clear engagement and active participation			
Pupils make effective use of visual aids and practical activities			
Pupils are motivated by challenge and inspiration			
Pupils show good progress by setting their own success criteria			
Pupils are engaged by exciting and imaginative lessons			
Effective differentiation allows all pupils to progress			
Questioning extends and challenges pupils			
Self-assessment provides opportunities for reflection and improvement			
Collaborative learning enhances attitude to learning			
Communication is developed through a variety of speaking, listening and writing tasks			
Independence is promoted through opportunities in the lessons			
Knowledge, skills and understanding is evidenced through teacher questioning			
Pupils use ICT effectively			
Numeracy competency is achieved through appropriate tasks			
Pupils' attitudes are aspirational			
British Values/SMSC: Evidence and reference to			

Student feedback form: senior school

Table 6.5 Revised pupil feedback form 2018/19

	Strongly Agree	Agree	Disagree	Strongly Disagree
My lesson is on time				
My classmates behave appropriately in this lesson				
I enjoy/look forward to this lesson				
My teacher is enthusiastic about this subject				
I am able to learn in this lesson				
We do a range of tasks in this lesson				
My teacher assigns regular prep/ coursework/ independent work				
My teacher regularly marks my work				
I feel that I am making good progress				
I can ask for help if I need it				
I feel I am understanding as a learner				
I feel positively challenged in this lesson				
This was a typical (normal or usual) lesson				

A junior school feedback form for Years 3 to 6 was created in 2015 and adapted over time to gauge the happiness of junior school pupils in their learning and the wider school environment.

Student feedback form: junior school (introduced in September 2015)

Table 6.6 Junior school pupil feedback form

	Strongly Agree	Agree	Disagree	Strongly Disagree
I enjoy learning during these lessons				
The work in these lessons is varied and interesting				
My friends are kind to me				
I can ask my teachers for help				
Behaviour of other children is good in these lessons				
I feel safe in school				
School is an exciting place to be				
I feel happy and supported int these lessons				
My teacher gives me the chance to work independently and in groups				
I am challenged in the classroom and given the chance to make mistakes in order to learn more				

Teacher feedback form (introduced in 2018/19)

Table 6.7 Teacher feedback form

	Strongly Agree	Agree	Disagree	Strongly Disagree
The lesson is on time				
My pupils behave appropriately in this lesson				
I enjoy/look forward to this lesson				
I am enthusiastic about this subject				
The pupils are able to learn in this lesson				
A range of tasks are done in this lesson				
I assign regular prep/ coursework/independent work				
I regularly mark pupils work				
I feel that the pupils are making good progress				
My pupils feel comfortable asking for help if they need it				
I understand my pupils as learners				
I positively challenge pupils in this lesson				
This was a typical lesson				

Results over time

For the past three years, the pupil feedback statistics have been consistent and show a significant improvement in the emotional environment within the classroom and a knock-on effect on behaviour within the classroom. Figures show averages for the three years 2016–2019.

What is interesting about Figure 6.2 is that the numbers have not changed over the past four years: pupils consistently report that their classmates' behaviour isn't good at the same rates. In every Stage 3 meeting I have had

My lesson is on time

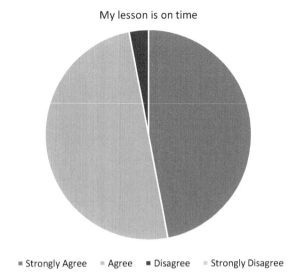

■ Strongly Agree   ▪ Agree   ■ Disagree   ▪ Strongly Disagree

Figure 6.1 Pupil feedback (My lesson is on time)

My classmates behave in this lesson

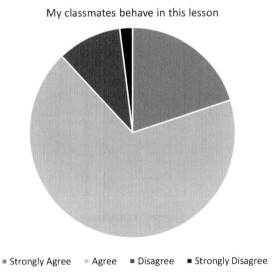

■ Strongly Agree   ▪ Agree   ■ Disagree   ■ Strongly Disagree

Figure 6.2 Pupil feedback (My classmates behave in this lesson)

My teacher is enthusiastic about this subject

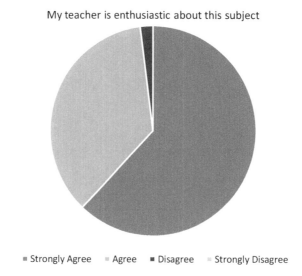

■ Strongly Agree ■ Agree ■ Disagree ■ Strongly Disagree

Figure 6.3 Pupil feedback (My teacher is enthusiastic about this subject)

I am able to learn in this lesson

■ Strongly Agree ■ Agree ■ Disagree ■ Strongly Disagree

Figure 6.4 Pupil feedback (I am able to learn in this lesson)

with staff over the past three years this has been a topic of conversation and we are quite baffled. The teachers don't see bad behaviour, nor the observers, and certainly not ISI when they inspected in April 2019 and commented on the excellent behaviour of the pupils. I have queried this with various groups of pupils over the past few years and we have also added to the form that

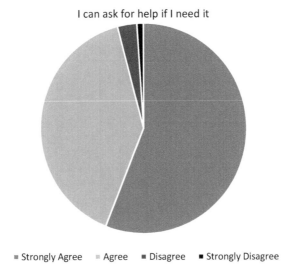

Figure 6.5 Pupil feedback (I can ask for help if I need it)

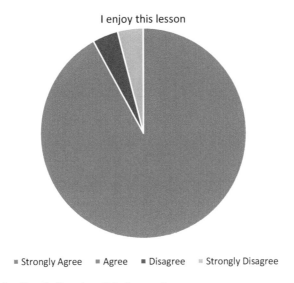

Figure 6.6 Pupil feedback (I enjoy this lesson)

the question of behaviour is directly related to the lesson and not outside the lesson, and yet these ratings are consistent.

The situation represented in Figure 6.7 looks bad but it's not. The data includes practical subjects where preparation is not set regularly, such as music, drama, and design and technology. If the question was not applied to practical subjects, the red areas would virtually disappear.

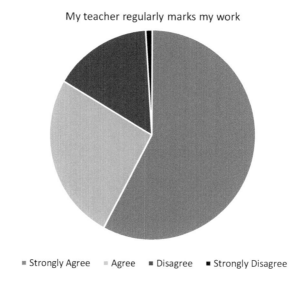

Figure 6.7 Pupil feedback (My teacher regularly marks my work)

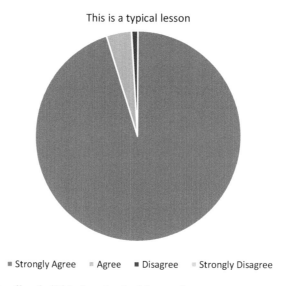

Figure 6.8 Pupil feedback (This is a typical lesson)

This is the most pleasing statistic (Figure 6.8) in that pupils feel that the quality the observer sees in the lesson is the consistent quality pupils experience in the classroom.

The focus within the forms above are merely suggestions; every school will have different areas for exploration. They do not need to stay the same each year, although our questions regarding emotional environment are still the main priority. In 2019/2020 the feedback forms for pupils and teachers correspond so we can gauge perceived differences in outcomes. The lesson observation forms can be as simple or as complicated as a school wants to make them.

There is nothing more stifling than rigidity in any system and, therefore, constant review, reflection and adaptation ensures this process remains fresh and relevant.

In conclusion

Stage 1 lesson observations are a privilege to be part of. Heads are often stuck behind closed doors dealing with problems and this process is wonderful in bringing us out into the school where we belong, and a great way to engage with pupils and staff. There is nothing more uplifting than to witness the wonderfully secure emotional environment of your school and the excellent learning that takes place. This atmosphere is infectious and reminds us of why we chose to be in the profession.

CHAPTER 7

Stage 2
Factors outside the classroom

In this chapter we consider the objectives and purpose of the Stage 2 meeting, how it is implemented, and the benefits and outcomes from this part of the process.

Outside the classroom, all teachers are responsible for effective planning of lessons in line with department schemes of work, tracking and monitoring of pupil progress using data to inform teaching and learning strategies, and providing informative and well-written reports for staff, pupils and parents. The fundamental housekeeping elements of teaching are key to a well-run and effective organisation where there is consistency across the department and departments as a whole. It is never surprising that care in these areas can slip down the priority list for some teachers and should be an area for continued development.

Who undertakes the Stage 2 process?

The school needs to decide who undertakes the Stage 2 meeting. Again, ideally this should be a member of the senior management team, or the whole team taking into consideration teaching commitments and whole-school tasks.

To ensure the process is completed in a timely fashion, as with Stage 1 lesson observations, time should be blocked out to ensure Stage 2s are completed allowing the process to proceed to its conclusion at Stage 3. Ideally, this is at least half an hour to allow for all areas to be covered and meaningful discussion to take place. For practical reasons the fewer people involved, the easier the process is to administer. Delegate the choreography of the meetings to a member of the administration team who can present in a table when Stages 1, 2 and 3 take place and diarise them for the team. There is nothing more frustrating for all involved than the process to be held up and take too long – with the loss of momentum the impact diminishes. After six years and experience of this lag, we are now down to one person observing and one person undertaking the Stage 2s. This person has an eye for compliance and can work their way through the objectives quickly and efficiently.

The objectives of Stage 2

Stage 2 is intended to aid consistency within and across departments. The recommendations of our previous ISI inspection in 2011 had been to ensure consistency in our middle managers and improve the standard and consistency of marking. Progress up to 2014 had been slow and painstaking, which can often be the case in a large school. This provided excellent and ongoing evaluation of development across departments. It wasn't just the HoD being asked about marking, prep, tracking and monitoring, use of data and the progress of particular groups, but all staff – a collective responsibility. During the Stage 2 meetings, if there were failings in any area, that member of staff would certainly be going back to their HoD asking why they were not being steered in the right direction or why information was not being disseminated – they didn't like departmental failings falling at their feet.

This undoubtedly keeps HoDs on their feet and as a result staff feel the process is transparent, fair and clear across the school and everyone knows what the expectations are.

Stage 2 meetings also give all staff a voice. Every school should be succession planning, so why hide away talented people with something to say? The next leader of the school could be locked away in a department somewhere with much to say, do and achieve.

What a Stage 2 meeting looks like

Stage 2 meetings are a one-to-one meeting with the nominated member of SMT diarised to take it. There are four sections to the meeting (documented below):

1. Assessment and marking
2. Preparation
3. Planning
4. Reporting and tracking

It can be very uncomfortable for staff if there are misgivings in particular areas.

Don't be too surprised by the findings in Stage 2 meetings in the first round or two. Despite staff nodding their heads in meetings regarding the use of data, it is amazing how many will not have the data in their mark books, or be able to explain how it is used or how useful it can be in understanding the dynamics of the class and identifying teaching and learning strategies. I don't think we would be the only school to have had a complaint from a parent regarding a teacher not seeming to understand the learning needs of their child during a parents' evening. Being able to track and monitor the progress of SEN, EAL and highly able pupils also proves to be a challenge, and this meeting requires staff to think about differentiation and how they can prove that pupils in these groups are making progress – something that inspectors are sure to ask staff if called for an academic interview.

As mentioned previously, marking was an area of focus following our 2011 inspection. We had a couple of frustrating years trying to bring departments in line with one another and therefore this was another defining moment in bringing in the three-stage programme where individual responsibility could be closely monitored and departments held accountable. As before, individual members of staff will quickly unmask ineffectual HoDs if they think their ineffectiveness is reflecting on them.

Workbooks can be scrutinised during the lesson observation if the time is appropriate. During Stage 1, the observer can walk around the class at appropriate times and take a look at the work, but it is also good for staff to bring examples of their marking to the meeting to discuss whether the marking falls in line with whole-school and departmental marking policies, and provides formative and summative feedback in how a pupil can make progress.

To ensure consistency, especially at Key Stage 3, departments were asked to create grading ladders and marking criteria for the front of workbooks so pupils and parents could see how progress was measured – something that becomes easier once GCSE grades are introduced in Year 10. This was a challenging concept for many at the beginning but it is a valuable tool for providing consistency in tracking pupil progress not only in the individual subjects but also across departments.

Resistance

At first there wasn't what I would call resistance, but some staff didn't quite understand on the first attempt. There was lots of 'Oh, right', 'I see', and 'I get it now'. I think many headteachers will recognise that no matter how many times a procedure or policy is put in place, it still goes over the heads of some staff, and there are those who choose to ignore it in the hope that it will go away.

The impact of Stage 2

Immediately, Stage 2 ensured that all staff became more conscious and aware of policies and procedures, and how they were live in their work. That is a tremendous feat in any school.

Within the first year, the frequency and quality of marking improved. There was evidence of more specific feedback and that pupils were asked to rework any class or prep work that wasn't good enough. We had seen in previous work scrutiny that there was also inconsistency in how pupils were commended for their hard work in the form of department commendations. Monitoring the use of commendation stamps was also a key area of focus in the scrutiny. Parental complaints about marking dropped significantly. Presentation of work improved, especially among those pupils who selectively varied the standard of their presentation from one teacher to another.

The setting of prep, and whether there is too little or too much, often raises its head as a topic from parents in any school. We provide prep timetables to departments with guidelines for each year group, and yet we have varying accounts from parents regarding the prep experience. This is by no means an excuse, but I feel it would be a common story in many schools that boys, in particular, are quite canny and minimise (as far as they can get away with) the time, quantity and sometimes quality of their work; whereas, in contrast, the majority of girls will not be satisfied with the first or second drafts of their work and not content until a colourful drawing or insightful diagram has also embellished it. This is something I have seen across all the schools I have worked in and in schools I have observed. The Stage 2 meeting is an opportunity to discuss gender issues within school and how they may be improved. Often, working parties have been born out of such discussions with interested staff identified at this stage.

We all know that the more experienced teachers become, the less planning they undertake, unless a new topic is involved. As a music teacher, I knew what stage my classes had reached in the syllabus, what they had achieved and where we were going next; our resources were consistent, reliable and available. No one wants to create unnecessary work for teachers. Junior schools require their short-, middle- and long-term planning, but this is often done in advance and repeated year on year. When observing as part of Stage 1, the observer will know how well planned the lesson is by the questioning at the start of the lesson about prior learning and context, the pace of the lesson and differentiation for different groups of pupils. A focus on planning during Stage 2 may be due to the observer having doubts following the Stage 1 observation.

Reporting was another huge challenge and frustration for the senior management team. The summary reports at the end of each term were often littered with grammatical errors, spelling mistakes, incorrect genders and other repetitive flaws that indicated much cutting and pasting or boilerplate statements drawn from a bank of standard responses. None are acceptable in any school. Pupils and parents share reports and it is pretty embarrassing for a school to be openly ridiculed for reports that share a lot of text. Whether parents are paying for their child's education or not, reports are an important measure of a child's progress and communication home to parents. Reports were often late, which held up the proofreading process and there was little regard to the knock-on effect it had further up the management line to get the reports out on time. Any issues regarding report writing are raised in this section. The standard of written English across any teaching body varies significantly, including those who themselves have a learning need or for whom English is a second language.

This raises the issue of how fussy schools should be with regards to writing reports. When does a fastidious obsession for traditional English grammar become too onerous? For example, one of our staff was pulled up by a parent owing to his American phraseology. This I anticipated as purely the chance for a personal dig at this member of staff rather than any dispute in the interpretation of what the report was saying, which in my opinion was fine. Staff from different parts of the country will have varying colloquialisms and sentence construction familiar to their region, which makes the report more personal and individual, rather than the thousands of reports sounding as though they were written for the shipping forecast. Stage 2 is an opportunity to discuss how reports are written and if any truly sloppy work is taking place, it can be addressed.

Stage 2 form

This form is used by the member of SMT undertaking the Stage 2 meeting.

In conclusion

Stage 2 meetings are invaluable in holding staff to account for all the technical aspects of their work. By challenging staff accomplishments in these

Table 7.1 Stage 2 form

Part 1: Assessment/Marking	Yes	No	Notes
Consistent with Department/Whole School Policies			
Pupils reflect on the marking			
Marking sets clear targets relating to learning needs			
Formative and summative feedback is given			
Student workbooks have marking/grade criteria stuck in the front			
Part 2: Prep	Yes	No	Notes
Set regularly (most weeks)			
Is sanctioned if incomplete or late			
Shows progression over time			
Inadequate or incomplete work is redone and marked			
Marked for spelling, grammar, punctuation and paragraphs			
Part 3: Planner	Yes	No	Notes
Planning is maintained and up-to-date			
Lesson plans how progression throughout a scheme of work			
Baseline data and SEN information is recorded			
Student progress is monitored against data			
Part 4: Reporting and Tracking	Yes	No	Notes
Under-performing students are challenged and reported			
Follows whole-school policies on tracking/ monitoring/reporting			
Interim/summative reports are completed on time			
Interim/summative reports are accurate			
Interim/summative reports reflect student progress			
Interim/summative reports track progress and inform planning			

areas, the school will have consistency of good practice across all year groups and will ensure staff are aware of key policies, procedures and expectations: the light goes on. But what happens if the light doesn't go on? On the rare occasion this happens, coaching and mentoring kicks in.

It might be the member of staff is asked to come back for another Stage 2 meeting to review progress in these areas, and that's fine as long as progress is being made. For those who are misguided enough not to deliberately make progress, this is when the issue can be passed over to the performance management process.

Stage 3
Wider contribution to school life

This chapter explains the rationale behind Stage 3, what it looks like, its objectives and the impact it has.

Once Stages 1 and 2 have been completed, the admin staff responsible for coordinating the meetings book the Stage 3 meeting with the head. Again, I block out an hour or two, usually early morning, lunchtimes or after school so as not to encroach on teaching and learning time or protected free periods. Paperwork and the feedback forms for Stages 1 and 2 are put into a file for the Stage 3 meetings. Usually, if there have been any issues in the previous stages, SMT has flagged them to me as they have happened.

The meeting doesn't have to be a long one but should take enough time to ensure the member of staff feels that all angles have been explored and any concerns discussed, and there is time to say thank you for the hard work and commitment they give to school, closing off the process. Ideally, although the policy states the time the process should take, in reality there will be other issues that delay the process, such as staff absence, fire alarms, and other unexpected events. Setting the unexpected aside, it should be no longer than three weeks from start to finish; otherwise the momentum is lost and the importance of the process diminished.

There is always opportunity for the conversation to be two-sided as well and bring the conversation around to the demands that headteachers and schools have and how staff can help. After all, state or private school, they are all run as businesses on a budget, and more often than not the demands and needs of the school outweigh the money available. Much falls on the goodwill of staff. Goodwill from staff is essential in providing the best outcomes for pupils because the time given for co-curricular activities is generally out of school contract hours.

Goodwill from staff will increase if the school environment and culture are good. It comes full circle: improve the culture and environment, more goodwill; more goodwill, better outcomes and improved culture. So what do staff contracts do for goodwill?

Actual contracts versus goodwill contracts

I have taken a reasonably wide-ranging view of suggested teachers' contracts across unions and other examples available online. They are pretty standard and technical, as one would expect with regards to terms and conditions. In state sector contracts, there is a focus on the set number of days and hours in the academic year that teachers are expected to work, although many teachers go above and beyond the standard expectation. It doesn't hurt to have an expectation of co-curricular involvement in the contract, especially in a fee-paying school where it is expected. As a teacher, I would want to contribute, especially as I am a musician and you rely on music staff to give freely of their time to get choirs and orchestras up and running, never mind putting on a show, when the hours are countless.

However – and this is rare – I have attended conferences where I've met teachers who work to rule and contribute nothing after the end of school, which is often 3pm in the afternoon. I find this hard to accept because it is the extra opportunities that schools provide for pupils that develop skills for life outside the classroom. In our school contract there is an expectation that all staff contribute at least one hour a week to co-curricular activities and, if on the Upper Pay Spine (UPS), in excess of one hour. It might be forgotten after many years since its introduction in 2000, but the UPS ('crossing the threshold') was created for those going above and beyond contractual expectations. Although not linked to appraisal, it is quite awkward if a member of staff on the UPS is not pulling their weight, and this one-to-one session is a good time to ask why. The quality of provision can also be assessed through this process. It could be that the knitting club is only attracting five pupils – which is great if those pupils value the time and it's a highlight of their week – but if just a gesture, maybe it's time to think of another activity. Poker became quite a popular activity in our school and, although a great skill, one needs to keep an eye on what is going on! Staff can be encouraged to offer an activity which is unusual, something of interest to them, and it can be refreshing for everyone involved. Staff value the monitoring in the programme because before the lesson observation programme, activities were not closely followed and the provision demands would always fall on the same people. As part of a member of staff's psychological contract, they will quickly compare the input that others give, weighing up their contribution to that to others, and this is an opportunity to ensure parity, consistency and fairness across the school.

Middle and senior management competencies

If the member of staff is a middle or senior manager, we will talk about management competencies such as exam results, departmental resources, choice of syllabus, developments in their academic field, departmental paperwork, leading by example and making an impact. Teachers historically have been promoted due to their outstanding classroom practice or contribution to school, and it shouldn't be forgotten that they probably have little or no business management experience. It is often good and excellent teachers who work their way up to be managers without such experience or training; others are brilliant managers but less effective in the classroom. Attempts over the years to keep excellent teachers in the classroom with various pay incentives probably haven't had the desired effect, because naturally ambitious teachers will want to climb the ladder regardless of pay (to start with). Management competencies can be as simple or as complicated as the school makes them. Search online for 'management competencies' and hardly two documents will say the same, so this form should be bespoke to your school and your expectations of your middle managers.

These are the competencies we discuss as part of this process.

i) Social, political and economic environment

Political changes always affect education, with new ministers, their zeal for sweeping reform, and the vast upset and expense that goes with it. On top that is the threat to the educational landscape which has been looming like the grim reaper for some years now.

> The threat of VAT on school fees and business rates relief is aggressively part of the Labour party manifesto and, until the run up to the 2019 election, more subtly within the Conservative manifesto. Although consciously missing at the moment, as it's not popular with its members, it doesn't mean it won't appear again in future. Independent schools have been fighting off this threat, primarily through the Independent Schools Council (ISC), with the Schools Together website promoting the incredible support independent schools offer to the state sector and

other areas of the community in terms of bursaries, resources and community projects.

With contributions from school under the Teachers' Pension Scheme rising to 23% in September 2019, independent schools are already feeling a big pinch and VAT could be the final straw for many fine institutions. The ISC has calculated that the damage to independent schools would have a far greater financial impact on the state sector than government realises, in a world in which it often can't get its own house in order. Why is it that 700,000 children received no work during the first lockdown primarily due to lack of devices and internet access, leaving teachers feeling impotent. This was further exacerbated by teachers delivering food, not lessons, to ensure children from low-income families were fed – an unacceptable situation.

In a statement on the ISC website on 13 September 2019, chief executive officer Julie Robinson stated the following:

> A punitive tax measure such as VAT on fees would ultimately hurt the country's education system, particularly state schools. As well as making independent school education an unaffordable choice for many families, smaller schools would certainly close, resulting in a sudden increase in the numbers of young people needing places at state schools – swelling class sizes and piling pressure on already-stretched budgets.
>
> Currently, 600,000 children are educated in independent schools, saving the taxpayer £3.5billion per year. These schools employ tens of thousands of teachers and support staff and a drop-off in the number of independent school pupils would result in staff redundancies. Along with job losses, there would be negative impact on many local suppliers, who rely on independent schools as part of their supply chain.
>
> In addition to not taking pupil displacement into account, the policy fails to address VAT recovery, something schools would become eligible for if it were introduced. Analysis by Baines Cutler shows that the policy would not raise money, but would end up costing any Government at least £416m in its fifth year and will not provide money to support spending pledges. There is a clear contradiction in a policy that aims to raise revenue from independent schools and reduce demand for them at the same time.
>
> Robinson (2019)

I've mentioned this issue purely because some staff in independent schools criticise management for being too corporate or driven by the bottom line. It is good for middle and senior managers to be aware of the dangers to the sector, and how our contributions are staving off government threats and keeping the school we work in viable. Political discussions and views on the social, political and economic environment will help managers assess risk in their areas, create SWOT analyses and keep their knowledge current.

ii) *Staff recruitment*

Staff recruitment is another increasing concern with many accounts of headteachers who have had zero applications for keys posts in maths, science and English. According to a Guardian article on 2 October 2018, an estimated 15,000 teachers leave the UK each year to join an international school, with a survey suggesting that 47% of teachers are dissatisfied with the British education system (Ferguson 2018). The 2018 Global Report on the International Schools Market undertaken by ISC Research states that there are a total of 9,605 English-medium international schools worldwide with Dubai having the greatest amount at 306 schools. If one looks at the websites of leading education headhunters, the majority of teaching jobs are abroad and offer significant financial reward. In the past two years, I have lost more staff to the temptation of life overseas than to UK-based jobs, and I've seen a significant increase in difficulty in recruiting highly qualified and dynamic staff.

iii) *Budget conversations and understanding*

It is also important the heads of department not only appreciate these difficulties but also seen the threats within their own departments. If asked to reduce budget costs, this is for a significant reason and every attempt should be made to look at current resources and the value for money they offer. Seeking the best value for the department ensures best value for the organisation. With increased use of technology, are classrooms still bogged down with expensive books, out-of-date resources like VHS recorders and copious amounts of paper? Is it time for a clear-out?

iv) *Leading by example*

Being a middle manager is difficult because you are sat in the middle: not only part of the departmental team but also representing and advocating for senior management decisions. Nobody likes a mood hoover. Negativity, cynicism and sabotaging behaviour can be insidious and spread like Japanese knotweed. Keeping your ear to the ground and carefully reading appraisals usually unearths particular disgruntlements that can be tackled head on in a Stage 3 meeting. Again, it's about being brave. You don't have to be controversial, aggressive or threatening, but raising the middle managers concerns brings them to the table and the wolf will often retreat back to its lair (until the next time). Regular Stage 3 meetings ensure that genuine grievances and concerns are explored.

Good middle managers inspire confidence and command respect if they are equally open, fair and consistent and show they are prepared to roll up their sleeves and not expect staff to do something they wouldn't.

v) Ability to lead and develop a team

Teamwork is essential, as explored in earlier chapters, for effective productivity as all members will foster different skills and characteristics. A middle manager leading the departmental team is no different to the headteacher in setting high expectations and leading by example. Again, teachers have an innate sense of justice and weigh up psychologically the efforts and contribution of other team members. Middle managers who don't have expectations of themselves and the team, and don't respect and identify diversity within the team and promote harmony, will have problems from their team and ultimately the head. How good is this member of staff at team-building?

vi) Planning and organisation

This is an opportunity to consolidate consistency across middle managers and to ensure the language used in the meeting expresses the common strategic vision of the school and is reflected in departmental documentation.

vii) Making things happen

As a head, you might find it frustrating that you have to initiate ideas and projects, and come up with resolutions and innovations. In the Stage 3 meetings over the past couple of years, I have asked middle managers how their departments are innovating. Innovation doesn't have to cost anything. Keep records of the ideas mooted in the meetings and follow them up. If every department comes up with one innovative idea, a practice or way of thinking, the school soon becomes more dynamic and inspirational. Stamp out 'can't do' attitudes and challenge the obstacles that stop innovation and stretch for everyone. Follow this through in assemblies and staff meetings so it becomes a culture across the school.

When assessing departmental progress – without telling experienced managers how to suck eggs – look at the value added and not raw results. Are middle managers proactive rather than reactive with those pupils who might fail? Are departmental procedures identifying issues that inform planning? Are middle managers being held to account for pupil progress in their departments or are they ready to blame someone else?

viii) Influencing and negotiating

Middle managers should be encouraged to barter with one another as well as the head and develop skills of persuasion and negotiation as well as compromise. In schools that have a high level of co-curricular activity, there is often conflict with enthusiastic teachers, most notably so with sports and performing arts departments. Often the same children participate in both activities and this often causes conflict between HoDs. How do they manage this potential conflict for the best outcomes of the departments but also the pupils?

Leaders have the responsibility to develop middle managers themselves into leaders. Identifying the middle leaders' management and leadership qualities is only possible if we are aware of what they are. Have you ever explored your own leadership qualities or scrutinised the behaviours and characteristics of your senior team? Knowing ourselves and others is crucial to successful change management and the implementation of innovative ideas, driven by the support of your team.

What it all means

Stage 3 is the real coaching and mentoring section of the three-stage programme in that it opens up a wide discourse on all aspects of contribution to school and management. As mentioned before, teachers often quickly get management posts due to their excellence in the classroom rather than any management experience, which could be zero. The Stage 3 is very much like CPD in nurturing managers and opening their minds to the wider issues school faces, preparing them for senior leadership.

Stage 3 – Management competencies

Table 8.1 Management competencies

Area of focus	Notes
Ongoing and up-to-date awareness of the demands on the organisation and its strategic vision	
Local, national and international environmental factors affecting business	
Effectively plans and maintains departmental budget	
Effectively plans and maintains capital projects	
Seeks and delivers best value for the organisation	
Leads by example	
Inspires confidence and commands respect	
Identifies and understands own leadership style	
Sets high expectations of themselves and others	
Respects the needs of others	
Takes pride in own work and is clear about accountabilities	
Fosters good working relationships	
Work is effectively planned and organised	
Department objectives reflect the school development plan and mission statement	
Resources are prioritised and scheduled effectively	
High standards are maintained across the team	
Departmental paperwork maintained and up to date	
Academic results reflect GL/CEM data and expectations	
Challenges and seeks opportunities for self and the team	
Inspires a 'can-do' and 'yes' ethos	
Demonstrates tenacity and strength	
Uses effective communication	
Contributes to team, departmental and SMT discussions	
A range of strategies used to shape and influence decisions	
Possesses high-level negotiation and compromise skills	

In conclusion

Stage 3 is an effective means of wrapping up the process and giving staff individual quality time to talk about the emotional environment, about their teaching and how well they are undertaking all aspects of what it takes to be an effective teacher. Appreciating the extra time teachers give to whole-school projects and co-curricular involvement really spurs on staff to give more. Taking time to know staff is great for succession planning and knowing where and how to develop staff in the future. Everyone has a voice and it should be heard and celebrated.

Part 3

Leadership
knowing me, knowing you

This chapter defines what leadership is, helps you identify as a leader and the measures you can take to find out if you have the right balance on your team.

Implementing a completely new programme and the change that goes with it means you need to know who you are, how you work and what characteristics you have that could hinder or completely destroy any good intentions you have to bring about change. Equally, you need to know what makes your team tick. Who are the personalities, who are your blue-sky thinkers, finishers and completers, and those with an eye for detail? Have you got the right skill sets in place to have the right person delivering any aspect of the programme? Take time to do this first; it will also flag up where your silent assassins and antagonists are.

Have you consciously set out to identify what type of leader you are? It may be that during the interview process for your current job, you undertook one of the many excellent psychometric tests that identified your characteristics as a leader. Do you feel you still relate to the findings of the test or have time and experience changed you? Do you understand how your behaviours affect others to the point where it may influence the success of change and innovation within the school?

What is leadership?

If one googles the definition of leadership, there are thousands of definitions. For the sake of simplicity, Lexico (the online Oxford dictionary) defines leadership as 'the action of leading a group of people or an organization'. What could be more straightforward than that?

Some definitions focus on the characteristics of leaders, others on attributes, some on success and what they do, but ultimately an effective leader will bring an organisation to superior performance through the success of individuals. As Richard Branson remarked in the Telegraph on 6 October 2011, 'Whatever your style, whatever your method, you need to believe in yourself, your ideas and your staff. Nobody can be successful alone – and you cannot be a great leader without great people to lead' (Branson 2011).

Leadership in the educational context also encompasses the ability to anticipate the future (Amanchukwu et al. 2015). Some leadership theories, such as the great man theory and trait theory, suggest that leaders are born with leadership qualities; other theories, such as behavioural theory, suggest that leaders are made, not born (Uzohue et al. 2016). My interest in this debate was sparked by Robert Plomin's book *Blueprint* (2018) in which he argues a person's blueprint is determined at birth due to DNA. It could be we are born with leadership qualities but our environment hasn't been conducive to nurturing these skills, but time, experience and training has brought forward these qualities.

Howes (1993) refers to *The Art of War* (attributed to Sun Tzu and written before 453 BC) and quotes the leadership guidance within this great work. *The Art of War* was first translated by a French missionary and its thirteen chapters have remained the most important military treatise for over 2,000 years. Tenets commonly drawn from the work include:

- Never lead by force.
- Know the competition.
- Doing nothing is better than acting out of fear.
- Always plan ahead.
- Refrain from decision-making when angry.
- Study the competition.
- Use your team wisely.
- Act like a leader.
- Trust yourself.
- Think strategically.
- Never lose sight of the group.
- Have a plan.
- Know when to quit.
- Know yourself.

Howes (1993) draws out another handful:

- Understand the nature of the problem confronting you: 'In a hundred battles, you will not be in peril'.
- Invincibility depends upon one's self, the opposition's vulnerability on him.
- Order or disorder depends upon organisation. To manage a host, one must first assign responsibility from the top to the bottom.
- Advantages and disadvantages are mutually reproductive. The enlightened will deliberate.
- A truly courageous man is cautious in the face of danger, one who deliberates before acting.
- Attain that which is possible, yet remember that even water will cut through stone over a period of time.

To simplify the minefield of theoretical literature on leadership theory and style, I will focus on three leadership theories most relevant to this book: situational theory, transactional theory and transformational theory; and three leadership styles as identified by Kurt Lewin in the 1930s: authoritarian/autocratic leadership, participative/democratic leadership, and laissez-faire leadership, plus paternalistic leadership as this often describes the leadership of school leaders and the problems it may cause.

1) *Transactional/management theory*

Transactional theory dictates that the leader removes all barriers to enable workers to achieve goals. Workers are rewarded when they succeed (pay increases, advancement and recognition) and punished when they fail. Transactional leadership relies on motivating workers through exchange and focuses on task completion and employee compliance. (Nanjundeswaraswamy and Swamy 2014).

2) *Transformational/relationship theory*

Transformational theory focuses on the connections between leaders and followers (Amanchukwu et al. 2015) and the process by which a person engages with others to create a connection and ensure the success of both individuals and group members.

3) Situational theory

Situational theory proposes that leaders change their leadership style according to the current conditions or set of circumstances as different leadership styles give opportunities for different decision-making processes.

1) Authoritarian/autocratic leadership

The characteristics of this leadership style include little or no input from group members into the decision-making process where leaders make all the decisions, dictating work methods and processes and group members are rarely trusted with decision or important tasks. This is often classed as the classical approach in which the manager retains as much power and decision-making authority as possible (Khan et al. 2015). There is little creativity or out-of-the-box thinking, and rules are important and tend to be clearly outlined and communicated. This style of leadership can impair morale and lead to resentment if ideas and solutions presented by skilled and capable workers are not taken into consideration. Autocratic leaders can be viewed as controlling and the lack of creativity in finding solutions can hinder progress.

An autocratic leadership style does have its positives, though: decisions can be made quickly, especially under pressure, and there is a clear chain of command and oversight. It can be highly effective if the leader is the expert in a small team of unskilled workers.

So, who do we know who is an autocratic leader? To name a few: Martin Luther King, not in his non-violent pursuit of his beliefs but in persuading others to follow; Napoléon Bonaparte, to have led an empire; Bill Gates is positively autocratic by being a quick decision maker; Ivan the Terrible was a paranoid tyrant who killed his own son; Hitler and his leadership of the Nazi Party; others include Vladimir Putin, Genghis Khan, Elizabeth I, and Donald Trump. In the right hands, an autocratic style can bring success and power. In the wrong hands, it can bring destruction, oppression and genocide.

In a nutshell, although there is a time and place for autocratic leadership, this style of leadership may present the three-stage lesson observation programme as dictat and be seen as a criticism of staff and current practices.

2) Participative/democratic leadership

The characteristics of democratic leadership are found in the ability to delegate responsibility to the team and facilitate participation in making decisions, empowering team members with the right resources and training to achieve their goals and take an active but equal part in the decision-making process, although the final decision is with the leader. Creativity is encouraged and good democratic leaders will be honest and intelligent, and have courage, creativity, competence and fairness. Democratic leaders inspire trust and achieve respect among the workers.

Democratic leadership is a proven successful and popular leadership style, although it doesn't come without its problems. Leaders may appear to be indecisive, especially in a crisis with little time to consult others. Being consultative can take time and democratic leaders find it hard to cut corners, often finding themselves apologising for not taking on board a suggestion from one of the team. Team members may feel that because they are being listened to, their ideas will be adopted, which is not necessarily the case and may cause resentment.

Indra Nooyi, the former CEO and chairman of PepsiCo, is a particularly good example of a democratic leader who endeared herself to the workforce. In implementing the three-stage lesson observation programme, knowing when to be democratic is crucial. However, too much consultation can delay the process when you have decided already it is going to happen.

3) Laissez-faire leadership

Laissez-faire leaders give very little guidance to the workers and provide the tools for workers to make decisions and expect them to find the resolutions to problems. Although power is handed over to followers, the leader still takes responsibility for the group's decisions and final actions. A laissez-faire leadership can be highly successful for teams with high expertise and skills, and creative teams that value independence. The downside is that it is no good for groups lacking skills, motivation and adherence to deadlines and may result in poor performance and outcomes. The leader may appear to be passive and uninterested.

Examples of laissez-faire leadership include Queen Victoria, whose leadership style reflected attitudes common during her reign: 'Heaven helps those who help themselves'; and Herbert Hoover, rightly or wrongly labelled the last stubborn laissez-faire leader in America, oversaw the Great Depression in 1929 with the laissez-faire economy and do-nothing policies.

In a nutshell, if you are a laissez-faire leader without the ability to adopt one of the other leadership styles at the right time, you could be in for a very rocky road. Unless, that is, you have strong deputy, a number two who can drive forward your vision for the three-stage lesson observation programme.

Situational theory proposes that leaders change their leadership style according to the current situation. Great organisations and, indeed, great leaders have shown that adapting their leadership has been instrumental in their success.

The reason why examples of democratic leaders are lacking above is because there many examples of celebrities who have embraced at least two if not three of these leadership styles, which has enabled the continued success of their organizations.

Google was founded by Larry Page and Sergey Brin while both were undertaking PhDs in computer science at Stanford University. Their success, apart from developing the concept itself, was in embracing all three leadership styles. Early on, they took advice and hired Eric Schmidt as an experienced CEO who adopted a laissez-faire leadership style, in contrast to their own autocratic tendencies: employing smart engineers, promoting them and leaving them alone to find the solutions. Although this was great to start with, they realised that not all employees thrived under this style of leadership and they gradually moved to a more democratic/participative leadership.

Steve Jobs also embraced all three leadership styles with varied success. In Apple's early days, in the late 1970s and early 1980s, a laissez-faire leadership style was appropriate because of high-knowledge workers in a new field, and the company thrived. Later, Jobs adopted an authoritarian leadership style and was forced to resign by the board. Ten years later when he returned, Jobs adopted a democratic/participative leadership appropriate to the maturity of the company.

Jeff Bezos at Amazon expanded his business by employing talent to create a democratic/paternalistic leadership model, but at the same time has been described as highly authoritarian.

J.F. Kennedy was a textbook charismatic leader but showed a laissez-faire attitude towards the Apollo programme and an autocratic response to the Cuban Missile Crisis, which required a quick decision.

In a nutshell, you need to be adaptable. Identify what characteristics you have, identify any weaknesses and work on filling the gaps. If you know your school and its culture, you will know when to adapt your behaviours.

4) Paternalistic leadership

Paternalistic leadership is a managerial approach involving a dominant figure acting as matriarch or patriarch and treats employees as though they were members of a large family expecting loyalty and trust. *The Godfather* comes to mind but I'm sure none of us would want to be associated with a mafia-like, tyrannical figure! Paternalistic leadership involves a focus on employee well-being and making decisions with employees' best interests taken into consideration. Absenteeism and staff turnover rates will decrease as emphasis is placed on employee needs, with good behaviour being rewarded. The downside to paternalistic leadership is that employees become too reliant on the employer, and team members become too competitive, vying for position with the employer. If roles are not defined properly and employees do not know what is required of them, there can be power struggles and internal issues.

Examples of paternalistic leaders include Henry Ford, who valued human capital, believed in equality and was emotionally intelligent. Ford raised wages to five dollars a day and reduced working hours to eight hours a day, realising this motivated workers and encouraged them to stay. José Mourinho is another good example of a paternalistic leader who could inspire others to achieve particular goals and motivate people to do more than they thought they could.

Pellegrini and Scandura (2008) suggest in their literature review that although paternalistic leadership is highly effective in non-Western cultures, it is criticised in Western culture as being likened to authoritarian leadership, although authoritarian leadership is associated with control and exploitation, and paternalistic leadership is focused on the care and protection of employees with loyalty and respect in return. The only real criticism could be the notion of inequality in the relationship.

In a nutshell, as the psychological contract with staff increases, there could be the tendency, over time, to shift to paternalistic leadership and the warnings above are quite clear. Balance is key. Think also of the poor person stepping into your shoes when you move on.

Ability to change and adapt

When I introduced the three-stage lesson observation programme in 2014, I had completed four years in post as headteacher. As explained previously, continued frustrations determined my authoritarian approach to its implementation. This was probably the second bravest thing I had done while in post. I can honestly say, looking back, that I didn't have a particular leadership style but, if any, I took an authoritarian approach mainly due to my lack of experience and also my desire to do things my way. As time has progressed, I have learned the many benefits of a more consultative and democratic approach to leadership but have the ability to be autocratic when needed. What I didn't realise at the time was that the programme, which created more interaction with the staff and the school as a whole, would forge and nurture change in my leadership style which after nine years is moving more and more to paternalistic leadership. There are warnings regarding developing a paternalistic culture in that dependency on the head can stifle the independence, growth and accountability of other potential leaders.

During the previous year, I had discussed with the senior team my ideas regarding lesson observation and we talked through and discussed the pros and cons of what could be achieved and the staff reaction to change. As usual with the democratic style of leadership, if you become too consultative there is a chance a decision won't be made and the new academic year was fast approaching. Plus, I had my own predefined ideas about what the programme would look like and didn't need or have time for any further input from the team.

Yasir et al (2016) explore different leadership styles with organisational change capacity (OCC). Employee trust is paramount in organisational change and different leadership styles at particular times in the journey can determine its success. The research suggests that a transactional/authoritarian style at the start of the process is negatively correlated to success, whereas a transformational/democratic style is preferable. Laissez-faire leadership is negatively related to OCC.

Taking this into consideration, you need to be sure where on your journey you are as there is much at stake: loss of management trust, governor trust, credibility and the risk of looking superficial and without substance. Unless you are far down the road of headship and have established a positive and trusting environment, an authoritarian or laissez-faire approach could possibly result in failure. You need to bring people on the journey through democratic leadership and then gauge at what point you might need to become more authoritarian as implementation progresses.

How do I know what type of leader I am?

Knowing who we are is crucial, as well as the impact we have on the feelings of others. Our self-awareness is paramount to success because until we understand ourselves, how can we understand others and how we can interact successfully? Psychometrics is a science of measuring behaviour or ability and, most usually, personality. Psychometric tests can be used to evaluate competencies, values, personality traits and intelligence. Questions relating to goals, forward thinking, and teamwork ability to inspire and motivate are quite revealing.

Warren Bennis, described by Forbes magazine in 1996 as the 'dean of leadership gurus' states that research at Harvard University indicates that 85% of a leader's performance depends on personal character (Bennis 1999). 'Every effective leader I've known is passionate about what he or she is doing. The time and energy devoted to work demands a commitment and conviction bordering on love'. (Bennis 1999: 20).

Understanding who we are and understanding others helps us appreciate that everyone is different, has value and special strengths and qualities. It is also helpful to know how others perceive you and react to your personality and style. Personality models extend back to Ancient Greek medicine and philosophy with references by Hippocrates (c. 460–377 BC) known as the father of medicine, to the concept of humorism in which four bodily fluids (blood, yellow bile, black bile and phlegm) are linked to personality traits and behaviours. Plato (428–348 BC) also refers to ideas about character and personality. Modern medical science has rejected the theory of the four temperaments, although they are still used as metaphors in certain psychological fields and have been the basis of much theorising by various psychologists over hundreds of years, greatly shaping our modern theories of temperament.

Carl Jung's theories on the collective unconscious and the identification of archetypes have been instrumental in the development of this field. Once a supporter of Freud, Jung's attitude types of introverted and extraverted feature strongly in many modern personality systems, including the pioneering Myers–Briggs test. The Myers–Briggs test developed by Katherine Cook Briggs and Isabel Briggs Myers became one of the most widely used self-reporting assessment tools in recruitment and leadership development programmes. Their research began during the Second World War, and initially was aimed to help women identify the wartime industrial work that would best suit them. Today, psychometric testing is estimated to be a $2bn a year industry in the US alone (Wilsher 2015) and reveals traits that tend not to show up at interview.

There are two main approaches to psychometric testing. The first is an ipsative approach, known as a forced-choice scale and used in personality questionnaires to assess traits and behaviour. Rather than ask an individual to rate a statement on a scale of 1–5, it presents a choice of two to four equally positive statements making the individual think more about their answer. No single answer in itself is more desirable or acceptable, avoiding the social desirability issue, and an ipsative test does not compare responses with other individuals as a normative test does.

Normative tests have the ability to explore personality traits by comparing the results to the responses of others, making this test measurable. Unlike an ipsative test, normative tests usually use a 1–5 Likert scale. However, the downside of a normative test can be that respondents answer in a fashion that they think the employers might desire to see rather than honestly, and they may also tire with the length of the test and respond flippantly to get to the end. Ideally, therefore, tests that are either ipsative or a combination of ipsative and normative tend to be more reliable.

There is an extraordinary market for psychometric testing, as indicated above, and there is a minefield of different tests for different situations. The Myers–Briggs Type Indicator (MBTI) is possibly the most well-known test, identifying four areas of preferences (rather than opinions), which elicit temperament and personality.

1) Extraversion or introversion: Where do you put your attention? Do you spend time in the outer world or the inner world of ideas and images?

2) Sensing or intuition: Do you pay more attention and give more energy to information that comes through your five senses, or pay more attention to the pattern and possibilities you can see in the information you receive?

3) Thinking or feeling: Do you like to put more weight on objective principles and impersonal facts, or more weight on personal concerns and the people involved?

4) Judging or perceiving: How you live your outer life and what are the behaviours others tend to see. Prefer a more structured and decided lifestyle or a more flexible and adaptable lifestyle.

From this there are a choice of sixteen distinctive personality types to choose from.

Integrated Leadership Measure: ILM72

The ILM72 is the result of a major study carried out by AQR International and the Institute of Leadership Management that looked at fifty leadership models. It found common characteristics across most leadership styles and identified six scales representing different aspects of leadership style.

1) Goal orientation: how important achieving goals is to the leader.
2) Motivation: what the leader believes is the prime path to motivation.

3) Engagement: How leaders will engage with others.
4) Control: The extent to which leaders need to be in control.
5) Recognition: The leader's preferred approach to recognition.
6) Structure: How important structure is to the leader.

'ILM72', AQR International (2017)

Core leadership competencies are identified as follows:

Determination to deliver: this describes a single-minded determination to achieve. Most satisfaction – the individual's and the followers' – is derived from this.

Engagement with individuals: this describes enhancing the capability, confidence and commitment of individuals to enable them to perform and to fulfil themselves.

Engagement with teams: the emphasis is on cross-functional teamworking – a leader knows and supports how people work together across the organisation.

'ILM72', AQR International (2017)

MTQ48

The MTQ48 is a 'mental toughness' questionnaire which is popular with organisations when appointing a leader because mental toughness is positively associated with performance, positive behaviour, well-being and aspirations. The four areas the test covers are:

1) Control
   i. Life control: I really believe I can do it.
   ii. Emotional control: I can manage my emotions and the emotions of others.
2) Commitment
   i. Goal-setting: I promise to do it; I like working to goals.
   ii. Achieving: I'll do what it takes to keep my promises and achieve my goals.
3) Challenge
   i. Risk-taking: I will push myself; I am driven to succeed.
   ii. Learning from experience: Even setbacks are opportunities for learning.

4) Confidence
   i.   In abilities: I believe I have the ability to do it – or can acquire the ability.
   ii. Interpersonal confidence: I can influence others; I can stand my ground if needed.

'MTQ48', AQR International (2017)

DISC profiling

Much of the theory behind DISC profiling was contributed by William Marston, an American psychologist who contributed towards the first polygraph and also created the character of Wonder Woman. Marston published his findings in his book, *Emotions of Normal People* (1928), and described four personality types: Dominance, Inducement, Submission and Compliance. The theory was developed into an assessment tool by industrial psychologist Walter Clarke and is now owned by John Wiley & Sons.

1) Dominance: Person places emphasis on accomplishing results, the bottom line, confidence. This person sees the big picture, can be blunt, accepts challenges and gets straight to the point.
2) Influence (Inducement): Person places emphasis on influencing or persuading others, openness and relationships. They show enthusiasm, are optimistic, like to collaborate and dislike being ignored.
3) Steadiness (Submission): Person places emphasis on cooperation, sincerity, dependability. This person doesn't like to be rushed, is calm in manner and approach, and supportive in actions.
4) Conscientiousness (Compliance): Person places emphasis on quality and accuracy, expertise and competency. This person enjoys independence, objective reasoning, wants the details and fears being wrong.

Baldino (2017)

These are just a few examples of some effective programmes on identifying your characteristics and traits as a person and as a leader. Not only will you understand yourself but also others and how to build good relationships with those around you. It takes a team to deliver change; one person alone will not implement healthy change and influence school culture. The word *culture* itself implies collectivism and collaboration. If a team cannot work together, you have met a brick wall before you even start.

I have had first-hand experience of DISC profiling through the work of Thomas International and my interest in psychometric testing over many years gained momentum when discovering the company's excellent work. Dr Thomas Hendrickson developed Marston's DISC theory further in the late 1950s and early 1960s to produce the Thomas Personal Profile Analysis (PPA).Our senior management team trialled the test and it was quite a fun and insightful exercise for us. From there, we trained twenty of our staff to provide feedback to pupils as part of their careers package. Engaging staff in the training so they could first understand themselves and then guide the pupils through the results of the tests gave the school body a sense of ownership and collaboration. The test identifies your personality type, which may be a combination of more than one. It also identifies how behaviour changes when under pressure.

DISC profiling can start constructive discussion, as I discovered with my daughter. Both of us tested to be high Dominance and relatively low Influence, which would explain why we came head-to-head at times. Under pressure, my Dominance would increase further but hers fell dramatically and Influence took over. I admit I can become quite obstinate while she becomes the more measured reasoner who nearly always manages to get her way – but quite fairly too. The test certainly revealed who was the more adult of the two of us under pressure. Seeing these results made us laugh and, ironically, whenever we did approach conflict we nearly always ended up laughing before any real conflict took place. Understanding each other certainly makes a difference.

Our school's relationship with Thomas International developed further when we adopted the Trait Emotional Intelligence Questionnaire (TEIQue) programme, which measures fifteen emotional traits and four broad factors: well-being, self-control, emotionality and sociability. The test can also be adapted for school-age children as well and this proved a valuable tool alongside the PPA.

> Trait EI is defined as a constellation of emotional self-perceptions located at the lower levels of personality hierarchies […] Trait EI is the only operational definition in the field that recognizes the inherent subjectivity of emotional experience.
>
> (Petrides 2010)

Petrides is the principal developer of the family of TEIQue instruments and has published extensively and lectures internationally on trait emotional intelligence, personality, psychometrics and individual differences. 'Trait EI does not assume that there is some archetypal "emotionally intelligent" individual whom all leaders, managers, and employees should strive to emulate in order to succeed.' Again, it is an opening to a discussion.

Know your leadership team

It's also important to know your team, as failing to understand differences will result in the decreasing productivity of team members (Al-Malki and Juan 2018).

As for identifying team strengths, Belbin's team roles is still very much a favoured method among leadership teams. The team role model is widely used in practice and in FTSE 100 companies, government bodies and consultancies. It has been translated into sixteen languages worldwide. The foundations of Belbin's research lies in the 1960s when Belbin and a group of associates carried out a nine-year study of managers across various organisations. In 1981 Belbin published his seminal work *Management Teams: Why They Succeed or Fail* and in 1988 established Belbin Associates with his wife and son. The reports from the test were still hand compiled by Belbin at this point, but such was the demand that the Interplace software was developed. One of the most important claims in Belbin's work is that balanced teams have superior performance (Meslec and Curşeu 2015) and team member diversity is key (Aritzeta et al. 2007).

Belbin's original management team model recognised the presence of eight individuals to start with and then a ninth later on. Due to management teams often having fewer than nine members, the secondary roles identified in the test are equally important to establish a spread of roles across the team. Belbin believed that a team of six members was most suitable for tackling a complex problem and that the most competent managers seem to be able to function well in both primary and secondary team roles (Fisher et al. 2011). The roles are defined as follows (text adapted from Belbin team role materials):

The Plant

…is creative, imaginative, free-thinking and generates ideas and solves difficult problems. They are the source of original ideas, suggestions and proposals. On the downside, the Plant may ignore incidentals and be too preoccupied to communicate effectively. The Plant could also be prone to being absent-minded or forgetful. In conflict the Plant tries to dominate and shows Machiavellian behaviours.

The Resource Investigator

…is outgoing, enthusiastic and communicative. They explore opportunities and develop contacts. On the downside, Resource Investigators can be over-optimistic and lose interest after the initial enthusiasm. The Resource Investigator could be forgetful enough to not follow up a lead, will attempt to take control despite not liking conflict but will look to find a compromise. They are highly emotionally intelligent and have an innovative cognitive style.

The Co-ordinator

…is mature, confident and identifies talent. They clarify roles and delegate effectively. On the downside, Co-ordinators can be seen as manipulative and they offload their own share of work. Co-ordinators can over-delegate, leaving themselves with little to do. Co-ordinators have an adaptive cognitive style, are highly emotionally intelligent and although they will attempt to take control, they will try to find a compromise in conflict. The Co-ordinator shows low Machiavellian behaviours.

The Shaper

….is challenging, dynamic, thrives on pressure and has the drive and courage to overcome obstacles. On the downside the Shaper can be seen as manipulative, prone to provocation and can offend people's feelings. This person could be perceived as aggressive and bad-humoured in an attempt to get things done. The Shaper will attempt to control and in conflict will try to dominate. They have an innovative cognitive style, are achievement orientated, low in emotional intelligence and reveal Machiavellian behaviour.

The Monitor Evaluator

….is sober, strategic and discerning. They see all options and judge accurately. On the downside the Monitor Evaluator can lack the drive and ability to inspire others as well as be overly critical. They can also be slow at making decisions. The Monitor Evaluator has an adaptive cognitive style.

The Teamworker

….is cooperative, perceptive and diplomatic. The Teamworker listens and averts friction. On the downside, the Teamworker is indecisive in crunch situations and avoids confrontation. They do not like making unpopular decisions. The Teamworker has an adaptive cognitive style and has low Machiavellian behaviours.

The Implementer

….is practical, reliable, efficient, turns ideas into actions and organises work that needs to be done. On the downside they are somewhat inflexible and slow to respond to new possibilities. The Implementer tries to avoid conflict, has high moral values and low intellectual orientation. The Implementer has an adaptive cognitive style and shows low Machiavellian behaviours.

The Completer Finisher

….is painstaking, conscientious and anxious. They search out errors, polish and perfect. On the downside, the Completer Finisher is inclined to worry unduly and reluctant to delegate. The Completer Finisher has an adaptive cognitive style and tries to avoid conflict. They have a low emotional intelligence and high moral value. The Completer Finisher could be accused of taking perfectionism to extremes.

The Specialist

….is single-minded, self-starting and dedicated. They provide knowledge and skills in rare supply. On the downside, the Specialist contributes only on a narrow front and dwells on technicalities as well as overload you with technicalities. The Specialist has an adaptive cognitive style, will try to dominate in a situation of conflict or use avoiding behaviours.

Use what you find out to ensure successful implementation of the three-stage lesson observation programme. These descriptors are for the preferred behaviours that we have, and the tests will reveal where manageable behaviours are, as well as least preferred behaviours. These behaviours can and do change over time. For example, ten years ago I was a Completer Finisher without doubt – but that's because I had to be. On reflection – and not to blow my own trumpet – but if I didn't finish the job and see it through, no one else was going to. Now Completer Finisher is my least preferred behaviour (relief!) and I am firmly comfortable in the Co-ordinator/Plant profile. As a Co-ordinator/Plant, it is natural that I would come up with this idea but then need to realise the skills of my team and how they take the ideas forward. Straight over to the Monitor Evaluator (the thinker), driven by our Shaper, taken to the Specialists, Implementers and ultimately over to the Completer Finishers. All the team need to address their Teamworker behaviour and adapt to drive through the vision and present as a united front. There's an important place for everyone in the process and everyone needs to feel their skills are utilised and their role important in its success.

Success is the result of the combined success of the team!

■ Watch out!

Machiavellianism is a key issue in team success. 'Team leaders and others responsible for the health of their teams might do well to consider just how much Machiavellian behaviour is allowed in their teams' (Macrosson and Hemphill 2001: 8). In this article Macrosson and Hemphill discuss Machiavellian behaviours also identified by Belbin and the influence these behaviours can have on the team. From the descriptors above, it can be seen that although the Co-ordinator, the Teamworker, and the Implementer show low Machiavellian behaviours, the Plant and the Shaper have quite marked Machiavellian behaviours. Hence, the relationship between the Plant and the Shaper is never likely to be harmonious but they would be very good across the table for negotiation purposes. 'Watch Shapers and Plants for deceit, guile and dissembling' (Macrosson and Hemphill 2001). The Shaper, with their ability to hurt people's feelings and strong potential to disrupt, would also need to be watched as this could drive the team apart. The Co-ordinator and Teamworker have extravert personalities and are therefore great at facilitating communication and coordinating processes within the group. (Meslec and Curşeu 2015). The Resource Investigator tends to be the optimist and can help the group believe in what they are doing.

Can you be assured your team have your back? No, you can't, but good intuition and keeping an ear to the ground will help. The three-stage lesson observation and its ability to build on the psychological contract with staff especially during Stage 3 will bring great rewards in terms of loyalty and staff wanting you to succeed. Although you must always be aware of potential troublemakers in the camp, and normally they are easy to spot, loyal staff will be a great source of information even when they emphasise 'the best interests of the organisation'. As headteachers, we put great faith into our teams and it is right that they are trusted, but being complacent and possibly gullible, relying on what you are told, can be disastrous. Listening is powerful and if you listen to enough people you will know when the messages don't add up. The difficulty, as we all know when we jump the management fence, is that sometimes it hard to completely do so especially when we have been internal appointments and friends with non-managerial staff.

It is easier if you have formed your own team, but often headteachers will come into a school where the team is already in place, loyalties and psychological contracts are already mature and established – and it is almost like breaking in. Headteachers shouldn't be afraid of difficult conversations and will be respected for it. If bad behaviour prevails, hit it head-on. It is handy if the employment contract or code of conduct has a clause regarding loyalty and behaviour of staff, and ending employment is always easier within the first two years of a contract. Don't settle for second best, especially when the member of staff is a potential saboteur – you and the school deserve better. It's not often a headteacher will say 'I didn't see that coming': your instinct and intuition will let you know before the facts do, although the Licensed Trade Charity's CEO, James Brewster, has often said that even those close to you will 'shit on you'.

Coaching and mentoring

It is also the responsibility of the headteacher to make the team commercially aware and recognise that sometimes decisions are tricky, but without a buoyant school, jobs won't exist. Coaching and mentoring are invaluable for newly appointed senior managers either through the Institute of Leadership and Management (ILM) levels 3, 5 and 7, which we offer our staff, or equivalent bodies. The Apprenticeship Levy is a really good resource to invest money into all staff including teachers through graduate or postgraduate courses. Staff who feel invested in will give more back.

The senior team will also have psychological measures of parity too and, without sounding flippant or patronising, it is no different to managing the expectations of your own children when it comes to fairness and equality. It is easy, though, for a member of the senior team to accuse you of not being fair when their own inadequacies are raised, which is an all too familiar story with children also.

When our newly formed senior management team took up post in 2010, we undertook the Belbin roles questionnaire and compared our results as a team of five. Although some of the traits that came through were identifiable prior to the testing, there were surprises. Discussing the results was a good opportunity to get our frustrations out on the table, though without appearing rude or confrontational. For example, one of the team was clearly a Plant and, as a secondary style, a Resource Investigator. Forever the blue-sky thinker, with boundless enthusiasm and optimism more suited to an inspirational after-dinner speaker, the rest of the team had the opportunity to air their frustrations at that person's lack of detail and planning in how to achieve such blue-sky ideas. You could see the Completer Finisher among us glare across the table at the source of all their anxieties (the Plant), their eyes boring into the Plant's head, asking themselves if the Plant knew how much detail was involved in seeing the project through and hoping there would be no more blue-sky thinking in that particular session.

The exercise itself, though, was invaluable in understanding why and how other team members behave the way they do. Every team will need a good spread of team roles and new ideas, concepts and resolutions would not be found without the creativity of the blue-sky thinkers. Understanding each other and supporting each other through playing to our own strengths and accepting our weaknesses enables us to build a strong, united team.

Trust your intuition

As team members left the school, new applicants were routinely tested for their leadership styles and team roles to identify the fit with the existing members of the team. However, in Bell (2013) Belbin himself acknowledges that HR is a valuable resource in the decision-making process and that often it is a wasted asset when decisions are made purely by line management with a superficial knowledge of underlying people issues. All the tests in the world cannot pick up on the intuition we feel when we meet someone for the first time, the chemistry of the team, as well as the cultural fit of the organisation, which is so important.

▊ In conclusion

Understanding your characteristics and those of your team will instil you with confidence in how and when to make changes. Bringing key leaders and managers along with you and showing that you understand their views and feelings is key to success. The fewer enemies you have, the more likely you are to succeed.

The more you and the school is prepared, the easier the climate for change.

CHAPTER 10 Being prepared

This chapter explores how we really get to know what goes on in our classrooms. Don't trust the messenger: you need to get out there yourself and make your own judgements.

So, you understand – or are on the way to understanding – yourself as a leader and the dynamics and working cogs in your team. You have a good idea what the culture of your school is; but can you – hand on heart – say you know the level of good practice throughout the school and how well prepared for change your school is? Understanding where you are right now and, especially, understanding where the misgivings are, will give you the passion and determination to put things right.

How good is the teaching in my school and how can I prove this at present?

Exam results and assessments do not prove the quality of teaching in school. This is especially true in selective schools where high-ability learners tend to be good independent learners, curious and determined to succeed. Excellent exam results are obviously good outcomes for children but is excellent teaching a contributory factor? To prove this point, one only has to look at the amazing results achieved by GCSE pupils in 2019 at Michaela Community School in London, where many pupils are from disadvantaged backgrounds. A report in the Telegraph on 22 August 2019 stated that 18% of exams were graded a 9 compared to the national average of 4.5%, and 54% of exams were graded 7–9 (Horton 2019). Despite being labelled the strictest school in the country, the headteacher Mrs Birbalsingh has proved that with 'tough love' and high expectations, all children can succeed. The article also emphasises the emotional environment aspects in school of eye contact, politeness and cheerfulness.

Whether an internal appointment or not, within a few weeks of leadership it will be obvious who the immediate teaching stars are in the school through watching and listening to staff and pupils. There may be also teaching stars who rely on their charisma and friendly relationships with pupils rather than their teaching potential and performance. The only way to find out is to go and look for yourself and not rely on others. Although it seems a little draconian and 'Big Brother', there is no harm in taking the staff list and ticking them off one by one, and although I do not agree at all in grading teachers in the classroom, a simple note of the quality of delivery in classroom is invaluable. Once done, it will be possible to write a summative statement for your eyes only in which you see the standard of teaching in the school. Some heads will have a relatively easy time with this and others might find that years of unaccountability, apathy, loss of trust and belief may signal the start of a tremendous project ahead. How emotionally healthy is the classroom and how happy are your staff, pupils and parents?

If yours is a school with senior and junior schools with a through-school ethos, it is vital that the head or principal is seen as being consistent throughout the whole school, despite any protestations that teaching styles, approaches and practices are different. It is quite common in schools with this structure that the junior school tries to pull away from the senior school, often citing a lack of understanding and being the poor relative. It is important that peer observations take place across both schools so staff understand the pressures and demands that are prevalent in all year groups.

In the three-stage lesson observation programme, you do not need to be a subject-specific specialist or age-related specialist to know when good teaching and learning is taking place. You also do not need to be a specialist to assess the emotional environment of the class. If you are emotionally intuitive, you will trust what you feel in the classroom. The Stage 1 observation foci are quite simple and straightforward, and much will be assessed on gut feeling and intuition when in the class. You will know when the classroom environment is effective, when the atmosphere within the class is happy, vibrant and safe, and when pupil and teacher behaviours are excellent. You will feel the energy and buzz that goes with the territory of effective learning.

Heads of department exam results meetings early in the autumn term also provide invaluable data. Heads of department should present their exam results by teaching group, including the baseline data as well as actual grade per pupil to calculate the value added for the individual pupil as well as the class. True success is within the value added and not actual results. This opens a discussion with the head of department regarding teaching and learning with specific groups. In junior schools, similar meetings with subject coordinators and Key Stage leaders identify key issues and attitudes towards pupil outcomes. All schools have children with specific learning needs and many have EAL pupils. Value-added meetings discussing pupil outcomes give valuable insight to not only the teaching by these teachers but the experience these pupils have across the curriculum. The same names will crop up in conversations, either negative or positive, to give you a flavour of the quality of teaching and learning across the school.

How consistent are the practices of my middle management?

You can't expect your middle managers to be consistent in their practices if they don't know what the expectations are. Chances are your managers progressed to their positions through their excellent teaching and general organisation, and have not received any dedicated management training. Most of their training would have been through observing their own managers in the past, whether this was good practice or bad. Setting expectations across all departmental middle managers is a starting point.

To advocate consistency across departments, senior management staff need also to be clear about their own expectations and those of others. It is quite common for large schools to have heads of faculty, although depending on the strength of each particular faculty member, can you be sure that information is being passed down consistently? Personally, I feel all heads of department should have a voice, receive direction from the horse's mouth and be accountable for the consistency of practice across the school.

Policies should be up-to-date and live working documents. Lengthy and wordy documents without relevance and parked in an electronic folder, will not be read. Some schools meet for 5–10 minutes before or after school a couple of times a week. Rather than this time being a stage for notices, why not present one of the policies in a short, factual, concise, no-nonsense 'performance'? It doesn't always have to be the same presenter, either; use the different personalities and characters within the senior team or staff in general to deliver. An example of how effective this can be is in the inspection process. An inspector may well ask a group of staff when they last read or were spoken to about the school's code of conduct. A memorable five-minute burst of early morning INSET will stick in the minds of staff much more effectively than: 'It's in the policy folder somewhere and I'm not sure when I last read it'.

Ensure staff fully understand what the policies mean. A prime example is the marking, assessment, tracking and monitoring of pupil progress. There may be a whole-school assessment and marking policy, but does everyone understand it? Does the departmental marking and assessment policy relate directly to whole-school policy? Do pupils understand how their work is marked and how they are progressing? How do pupils know they are making progress? Schools across the country will use various practices for tracking and monitoring, but is this the work of one person in the school who turns this data out for inspectors, or is it department-wide where HoDs are responsible for proving the progress of their pupils? Policies are living, breathing documents and not just text on a page; they are meaningless without the content being the lifeblood of the school. Policies lay out the expectations of staff and, therefore, the outcomes of Stages 1, 2 and 3 will have real relevance to the nuts and bolts of how your school works, and you can gauge the effectiveness and success of these polices through the process.

Each individual department should be a mini business within the business, with its own development plan, up-to-date schemes of work, tracking and monitoring data, budget control, quality assurance measures and accountability. SWOT (strengths, weaknesses, opportunities, threats) and PESTLE (political, economic, social, technological, legal, environmental) analysis will also help managers in particular understand the challenges their particular department faces and feed this information to the school-level SWOT and PESTLE analyses to inform planning. Every school, no matter its size, is a busy and demanding place to work, but there is no reason why departmental meetings cannot happen at least every two weeks and the minutes submitted to a central location. Key agenda items should appear in every meeting, starting with the two most important items: safeguarding, and health and safety; followed by teaching and learning. Too often, departmental meetings are reduced to information dissemination (important, of course, because we need to communicate), rather than opportunities for challenging and thought-provoking discussions about teaching and learning.

I mention SWOT and PESTLE in particular as departmental exercises because all schools, state and private, are businesses and there is nothing more frustrating for a head than the lack of staff understanding that money doesn't grow on trees. An appreciation of the wider environment is invaluable: decision-making is less erratic and forward planning more efficient.

The survival and success of our schools depend on our collective reactions as staff in response to these environmental factors. At the moment it is literally the survival of the fittest and the challenges ahead for any political party are considerable: a UK and global recession, the COVID-19 pandemic and Brexit. Many of the strengths, weaknesses, opportunities and threats are unknown in our present political climate and there is no longer the level of predictability we once had. All teachers will have sensible and well-thought-out ideas and opinions that can create a highly effective development plan embracing future changes. Strength in numbers and a collective vision and mission are powerful.

Talking to staff during Stage 3 and hearing individual staff views will make the staff body feel valued and listened to. If nothing comes of a particular conversation, what you will learn is the level of interest of staff and who to call upon when certain working parties are set up. By talking and discussing school processes and practices as well as environmental issues, you can shape the consistency of practice across the staff body and gauge where work needs to be done.

Wrap the lesson observation in other teaching and learning practices

a) Peer Observations

The three-stage lesson observation programme needs to be wrapped in other practices to be totally successful. If one person is undertaking the lesson observations across the school, they obviously will not have the subject-specific expertise to evaluate the pedagogical aspects of the lesson, but as explained, Stage 1 in this process gauges the temperature of the emotional environment, classroom management and the nuts and bolts common to all teachers. However, staff need and want more theoretical challenges to their teaching and learning, and these can be in the form of departmental peer observations and cross-department peer observations. Setting up a formal timetable of observations will ensure they are carried out, as it is common for observations to be the first thing to go in a busy day. The deputy head in charge of academic (or equivalent) can monitor this and gain feedback from the observer and teachers who were observed.

b) Learning walks

Learning walks are also invaluable and far from being just another whip to take teaching staff unawares, they give teachers the opportunity to briefly observe the practices of other staff and open up discussions. Effective learning walks will be scheduled in advance with calendar invitations to all staff, including support staff and technicians to be really inclusive. Give a named focus for each learning walk and make it interesting and even unusual or amusing, as staff and pupils enjoy being part of learning walks – they are a great opportunity to break down barriers.

Separate the programme from appraisal and performance review

Ensure that all performance-related observations and paperwork processes are separated from the three-stage lesson observation programme. This is the time to revisit your appraisal process and possibly incorporate the HoDs' observations, but there should be no reference to Stages 1–3 unless there was something so drastically wrong that it would be unprofessional and neglectful not to report the issue.

Ensure everyone is aware of their responsibilities and their part in the process

Make sure you are prepared and have the resources to carry out the Stages in good time. Over the years we have been doing this, we have noticed that if you spread the task too thinly, there is a chance the process will slow beyond being practical. Use administrative support to book the Stage 1 observations, and Stage 2 and Stage 3 meetings in advance with pre-allocated diary slots determined at the start of each term. A hold-up at Stage 2 will obviously have a knock-on effect for the head at Stage 3, when pressing diary commitments will further delay the conclusion of the process, and this isn't fair on staff. The process itself and how it can be changed and adapted is addressed in the following section.

Project plan

Obviously, this will vary according to how far along the journey the school is, its current culture and the leadership style of the head delivering it.

A starting point is for the head is to produce their own risk assessment of what they want to achieve and the possible barriers to implementation, considering the 'what ifs'. This would inform the head's timeline for the project plan, taking into consideration:

1. Do I know myself? If you know your weaknesses you can mitigate before someone else finds them.

2. Do I know the team? Team-build to understand that diversity is a strength. Identify any saboteur – even silent ones can't completely cover their disdain. Be one step ahead.
3. Do I have the confidence of the team? I can guarantee you won't have full backing from your team simply because of human nature and competition.
4. Do I know my staff? I have been out in school and seen for myself?
5. Will heads of department see this as an intrusion or lack of trust?
6. What is the temperature of the common room? Are there politics to contend with, mainly through pockets of resistance to management?
7. What are the sorts of comeback from staff you might expect? Have an answer ready.
8. Who will carry out Stage 1 and Stage 2, and how can you guarantee consistency?
9. Is there administrative support in place to record and monitor the progression of the three stages?
10. In a large school with over 1,000 pupils, is this manageable? If yes, what does it look like?

Two terms of preparation is not unreasonable, starting with the fact-finding, data collection and risk assessment, and then presenting to senior management by the end of the first term. Bear in mind that even senior managers do not like change, so it's how you paint it. Like a good salesman, identify their common frustrations regarding teaching and learning, narrow down the priorities and then say you have an answer to all the problems! At least you might have a quiet room for a few minutes before the questions start. With different personalities and characters, the responses will be different but you can second-guess their responses.

Be assertive, be brave, be courageous

Once you start, don't waver! There will come a time when the democratic leader in you needs to hide and usher in the authoritarian. Senior management may falter from possible backlash from staff, but the party line has to be that the decision has been made and you are going ahead with it. Don't let staff threaten you with unions; you will be surprised how supportive unions are in recognising the demands made on heads. The three-stage lesson observation programme does not break any unwritten rules or myths about what can be done and can't be done in schools. Even with the Stage 1 learning walks and departmental observations, it is highly unlikely you will exceed the recommended three-hour guideline stipulated for observations across many of the unions. You do not have to bow down to unions either, but it is good to maintain balanced and respectful relationships. You have the right to lead and manage your school in the best way you see fit to achieve successful outcomes for pupils. If there are casualties along the way, what were they afraid of? If you find yourself wavering, revisit why you are on this path. You are here because you want the best outcomes for your pupils. Excellent teachers are confident and love to show you what they can do. How many teachers feel left out if they haven't been observed during an inspection? Most do!

Staff will admire your tenacity if you work with conviction, passion, clarity, accuracy and respect.

Be reflective

Reflect on the process every year as a team. Discuss what went well and what didn't work so well. Use the Stage 3 sessions to ask staff what they think and what they see as current and future issues that need to be addressed. Each school is different and will have different needs and wants year on year.

Over the past five years, the emotional environment in the classroom has remained our primary focus, but how we delivered the programme and by whom has changed many times. Observations have gone from HoDs alone, to HoDs and SMT, SMT alone, and then to me solely as principal. Stage 2s have been undertaken by all SMT and then to the new position of head of compliance for 2019/20. Stage 3 meetings have always remained with the principal. Bringing forward new talent and succession planning could involve engaging other staff in the programme, and the ability to be reflective and brave enough to change direction will ensure the continued success and respect of the programme.

In conclusion

Knowing your school and where it is right now provides you with the data to know where to start and the confidence to proceed. What barriers do you need to overcome? Data is key: having the facts, figures and evidence allows you to present the vision with credibility and conviction.

11 Presenting the vision

This chapter addresses and gives guidance on how the three-stage lesson observation programme can be communicated to staff. It is important to have 'all your ducks in a row' to ensure questions and challenges can be robustly justified.

It is important to communicate the vision collectively to all staff, including those schools that have different organisations (junior school, infant school, nursery school) under the same principal. This gives a clear vision that the three-stage lesson observation programme applies to every part of the school and all staff will be treated equally, with the same principles, practices and outcomes expected across the school.

The thought bubbles below are the slides presented prior to introducing the programme in 2014. A rationale for each one is included.

The bullet points post 2014 were added for the Wellington Festival of Education in June 2018 and for the benefit of readers taking into consideration further research since we launched the programme. What was quite striking is the amount of research undertaken post 2014.

Current issues regarding lesson observation

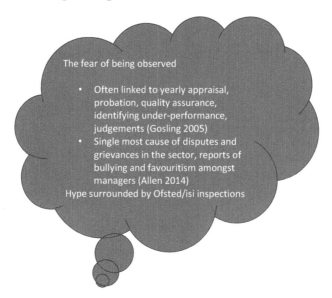

The fear of being observed

- Often linked to yearly appraisal, probation, quality assurance, identifying under-performance, judgements (Gosling 2005)
- Single most cause of disputes and grievances in the sector, reports of bullying and favouritism amongst managers (Allen 2014)

Hype surrounded by Ofsted/isi inspections

Figure 11.1 Fear of being observed

Theoretical background to change

Staff needed and welcomed as much background as possible to explain why observation was changing, in part because of the nature of the common room at the time and because there was such a vast difference to current practice. Academic staff appreciate well-documented theory and practice being brought into decision-making; it lends credibility to the decision to change. The negative connections between appraisal and performance management, combined with the bad press the inspectorates were having at the time, meant this struck a chord with staff and paved the way to a new lesson observation programme, purely for the sake of identifying good practice and celebrating it. My aim was to take away the fear of lesson observation and for it to become embedded within everyday school life.

I explained the criticisms of current lesson observation practice and the negativity it attracted.

If previous inspections have highlighted particular areas for improvement or made recommendations, or school surveys or complaints have brought to light particular areas of concern, this is a good opportunity to add them in. It is good to be humble and candid in explaining that maybe progress hasn't been as forthcoming as expected for a number of reasons, and that because the staff collectively want to be better, now is a good opportunity.

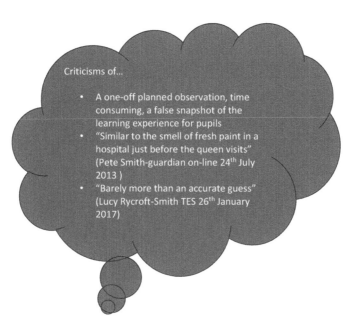

Figure 11.2 Criticisms of…

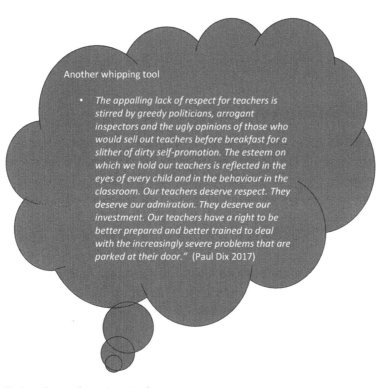

Figure 11.3 Another whipping tool

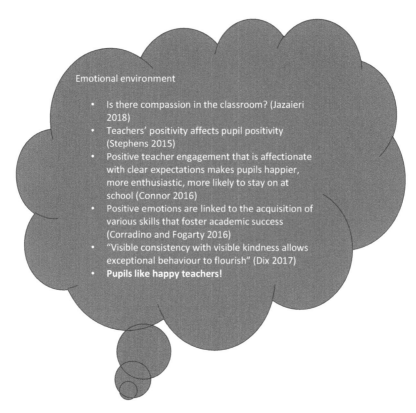

Figure 11.4 Emotional environment

Emotional environment of the classroom

Tangible areas for development are much easier to focus on than the emotional environment. This is a good opportunity to recount how people have made you feel in the past, both at school as a child and as an adult. Again research in this area is continuing to grow, more so than when the three-stage lesson observation programme was first introduced in 2014. Staff appreciate academic research that backs up one person's view on what should happen in the classroom.

It is important that staff understand they are in a safe place to be themselves, and that the school is not one-size-fits-all: diversity is embraced. They should be able to enjoy teaching in an effective learning environment.

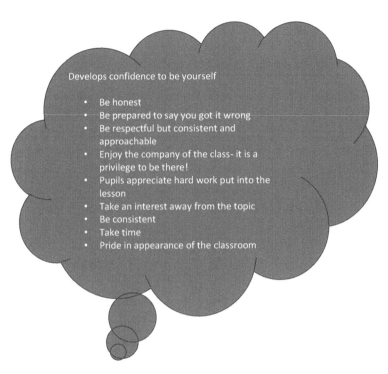

Figure 11.5 Develop confidence to be yourself

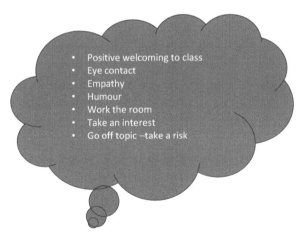

Figure 11.6 Positive environment

Be confident to be yourself

As an observer in my school or other schools, I admire teachers who can embellish on a topic and go off-piste with an idea or concept – this is how we learn. Why not, when studying Wagner, look into his political activities and compare and contrast the issues within Germany at that time, and the turmoil of the following fifty years or more? As long as the end result is that all objectives are covered, does it matter how we get there? More important is the quality of the journey.

All of this boils down to confidence: confidence to be yourself, confidence to break the mould – and to admit when things go wrong.

I have observed lessons of new members of staff who have come from schools where there was an expectation for all lessons to be delivered in the same rigid format. Staff feel comfortable and protected within this format, but pupils feel trapped and bored by the monotony of delivery. Having the confidence to deviate from the plan, go off-piste and speak with passion inspires pupils and creates the awe and wonder all headteachers want to see.

There is room for everyone: be yourself

A diverse common room is a rich commodity. No one should expect a one-size-fits-all regime. I call it a regime because one-size-fits-all would be like an army parade or worker ants. Diversity and different character types are so wonderful and should be celebrated. Learning to understand one another and learning to laugh together is invaluable. There will always be the 'legends' in the staffroom who get the loudest applause, but what I have observed over the years is how the legend is perceived by pupils and changed over time. The most applause hasn't always fallen on the loudest, cheekiest, fun-loving staff but often on the quirky, quiet and unassuming: the quiet bringer of excellence.

I don't like mediocrity and there is no place for it in front of our children. When stubborn mediocrity becomes a deliberate practice, it's time that member of staff left the profession. Mediocrity can be challenged and sometimes staff need to just know what excellence looks like. They might have been in a school where mediocrity was good enough or just not mentored towards the right direction. There is nothing more rewarding than to see, from one Stage 3 meeting to the next a year later, a member of staff really thriving after encouragement, and bringing them forward as an example of good or excellent practice.

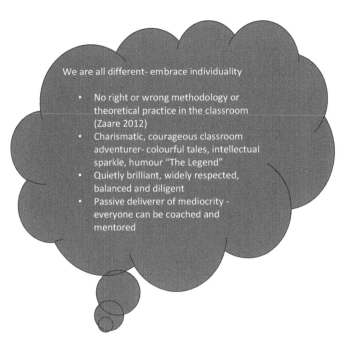

Figure 11.7 We are all different

Time for change

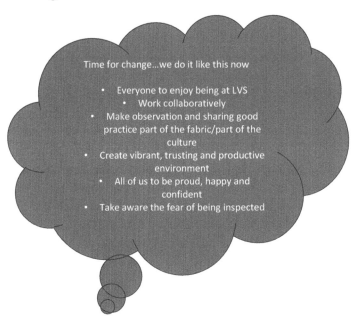

Figure 11.8 Time for change

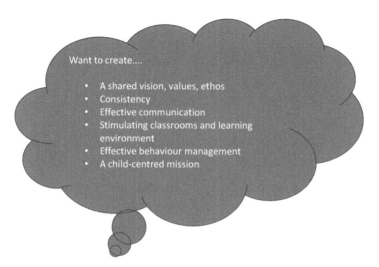

Figure 11.9 Let's create

Let's create

This slide emphasises that the change is positive and the outcomes for everyone are better. This is a good opportunity to really show passion for the objectives and outcomes of the programme. It's a very positive and empowering slide if delivered in the right way. It says that the staff are already good but could be excellent, pulling together and being part of a new initiative that will benefit all staff and outcomes for pupils

The three-stage lesson observation takes the best of the developmental and collaborative models (Gosling 2002), but mitigates any risks by a clear structure, consistency, accountability and expectations across the staff. Pupil feedback forms also provide a good control and checking system against the observers' and teachers' perceptions about what is occurring in the classroom.

A positive and effective emotional environment cannot just be switched on. It is the result of continued good practice and good relationships over a period of time. A key criticism of planned lesson observations is that they are not typical and pupils in particular can see through this. Pupils are asked in their feedback forms whether the lesson is 'typical' or 'as normal' and, as we know, pupils can be brutally honest!

What do pupils think?

It is important to gauge the feeling of pupils. After all, they are the customers. Canvassing the opinion of pupils is great at strengthening the pupil voice

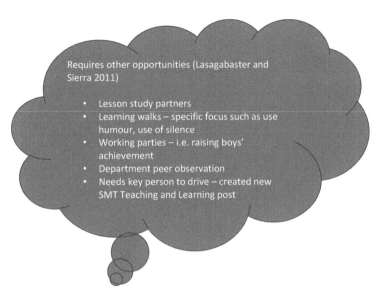

Figure 11.10 Requires other opportunities

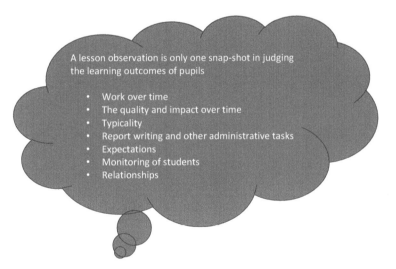

Figure 11.11 One snapshot

and making them feel engaged in their education. Children can be quite cutting and direct, especially when they perceive a lack of consistency or justice, but on the whole they are truthful and supportive of those who give their best to them. When I surveyed pupils' feelings regarding teaching and learning, overwhelmingly – and surprisingly at the time – came the response that pupils highly value the time and effort teachers put into the preparation

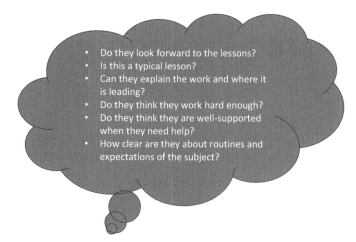

Figure 11.12 What do pupils think?

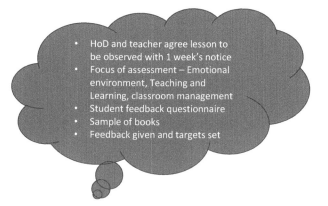

Figure 11.13 Stage 1

of their lessons. Pupil feedback is powerful, and it is also an important part of the pupil voice, which is highly regarded in inspections.

Stage 1

Note: In the first year, a week's notice was given for the observation; from the second year, no notice was given.

Stage 2: factors outside the classroom

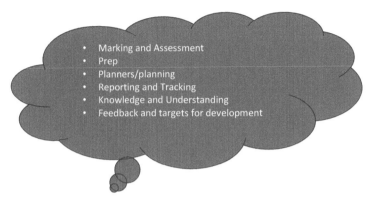

- Marking and Assessment
- Prep
- Planners/planning
- Reporting and Tracking
- Knowledge and Understanding
- Feedback and targets for development

Figure 11.14 Stage 2

Stage 3: Summary meeting

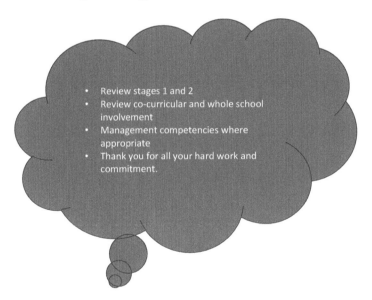

- Review stages 1 and 2
- Review co-curricular and whole school involvement
- Management competencies where appropriate
- Thank you for all your hard work and commitment.

Figure 11.15 Stage 3

In conclusion

Clear presentation and conviction in what you are proposing can be very inspiring and you may be surprised by the responses. Staff will appreciate the background work you have put into this and research will add weight to the academic argument that every academic looks to for validation.

Part 4

CHAPTER 12

Using the three-stage lesson observation data to build the self-evaluation form (SEF)

This chapter explores how the evidence and data collected during the three-stage lesson observation programme does not have to be lost but can inform all manner of official documents.

Every year, schools are tasked with policy review and updating of the self-evaluation form (SEF), two of many quite onerous tasks in a busy school schedule, especially if undertaken at the beginning of a new academic year. Continuous self-evaluation and reflection is good practice and should be the work of the whole staff not just the head or senior management. The three-stage lesson observation programme provides valuable sources of evidence to self-reflect, discuss outcomes and build the SEF. In September 2018, with the eight academic and other achievements and eight personal development areas of focus in quality of education inspections now appearing in the SEF, we linked these areas into the Stage 1 observation. We also distributed the SEF to the staff by department to add in and enrich the evidence we had already pulled from the previous year's observations.

A good SEF can be extremely powerful, not only clearly flagging to inspectors how schools perceive and evidence their success, but also as a marketing tool. There are a significant number of schools that, possibly because inspection is some way off, use their own self-evaluation to promote their good work and suggest possible outcomes of an inspection. For those prospective parents who are not clued up on inspection or understand the finer details, this could appear quite official and impressive. For recruitment purposes, this sends out the right positive messages that potential applicants want to see and starts off their psychological journey with the school on the right foot.

ISI educational quality inspections

Pupils' academic and other achievements

The quality of pupils' academic and other achievements focuses on:

A1: Achievements in examinations and external tests, pupils' progress and differences in the achievements of different groups.

A2: How pupils develop their knowledge, understanding and skills across the different areas of learning (linguistic, mathematical, scientific, technological, human and social, physical, and aesthetic and creative education).

A3: How pupils develop their communication skills (speaking, listening, reading and writing).

A4: How pupils develop their competence in numeracy, and how well they apply their knowledge and skills in mathematics to other areas of learning.

A5: How pupils develop their competence in information and communication technology (ICT), and how they apply their ICT skills to other areas of learning.

A6: Pupils' study skills and the ability to draw on a suitably wide range of sources. The ability to analyse, hypothesise and synthesise. How effectively pupils apply their learning and thinking skills to other areas.

A7: Pupils' achievements in scholarships and competitions, other academic distinctions, and success in sports, the performing and other arts.

A8: Pupils' attitudes towards learning. To what extent they demonstrate initiative and independence. To what extent they are willing to work collaboratively and to take leadership in their learning.

Contributory factors relate to the curriculum and how it promotes achievements and learning skills, and the significant aspects of teaching that promote pupils' learning and achievements. Other factors are the contribution of boarding, and leadership and management.

Quality of pupils' personal development

P1: How pupils improve their own learning and performance to build understanding, self-esteem, self-confidence, self-discipline and resilience.

P2: How good pupils are at making their own decisions and the importance of making good decisions.

P3: How pupils demonstrate their spiritual understanding and appreciation of the non-material aspects of life, whether religious, philosophical or other.

P4: To what extent pupils are able to distinguish right from wrong, understand and respect systems of rules and laws, and accept responsibility for their own behaviour, including their behaviour towards others.

P5: To what extent pupils are socially aware and able to work effectively with others. How well they work with others to solve problems and achieve common goals.

P6: To what extent pupils fulfil their responsibilities and contribute positively to the lives of others, within the school, including boarding, to the local community and wider society.

P7: How pupils show that they respect and value diversity within society, have respect for and appreciation of their own and other cultures, and demonstrate sensitivity and tolerance to those from different background and traditions.

P8: How good pupils' knowledge and understanding are of how to stay safe and to be physically and mentally healthy, particularly in terms of diet, exercise and a balanced lifestyle. How well they put this knowledge and understanding into practice.

Contributory factors, as well as reference to boarding, pastoral systems and leadership and management, make reference to how the curriculum, such as PSHE, promotes pupils' personal development. The three-stage lesson observation programme can also be used to observe PSHE.

New Ofsted framework: September 2019

The changes to the Ofsted framework took place in September 2019, introducing a much-welcomed quality of education section into the inspection and the separation of behaviour and personal development into their own separate sections.

- Inspections to focus on what the children actually learn rather than results.

- Designed to discourage culture of 'teaching to the test'.

- New 'behaviour' judgement to give parents reassurance on bullying; and 'personal development' to focus on resilience and confidence-building through extracurricular activities.

The focus of the new Ofsted framework mirrors that of the ISI framework in that there is far more emphasis on the outcomes for pupils, although it seems that Ofsted is going a step beyond ISI, which is refreshing and encouraging. The focus is now on providing a broad and rich curriculum and 'real learning'. The concepts of off-rolling (encouraging parents to withdraw their children before exams to enhance the data returns) and gaming (entering pupils for unsuitable qualifications to again enhance a positive data return) are under scrutiny and will have implications for any schools caught doing this. In 2019 61,000 pupils were removed from school rolls without explanation by the time the GCSE exams began (Woolcock 2019), with the largest numbers of those pupils being vulnerable or from larger multi-academy trust schools.

Criticisms of the new framework are widespread: the profession does have a reputation for never being happy with what it is dealt. Among the criticisms are that the target of 90% of pupils achieving the English Baccalaureate (EBacc) by 2025 is unreachable, especially due to the shortage of teachers with specialist subject knowledge such as modern foreign languages; and that funding, class sizes and the ongoing issues around teacher workload have not been addressed. I believe that the introduction of quality of education to the framework can only be a positive move and is child-centred rather than focused on data and teacher performance.

What is evident, though, and has been apparent for many years, is the conflict between the teaching profession and the inspectorates there to regulate it. There is much bad behaviour on both sides: teachers are in fear of judgement and, therefore, quite defensive and at times militant against the inspectorates; and inspectors themselves sometimes do not act in the supportive manner they should. The behaviour needs to change to ensure that schools and inspectorates improve their relationship to provide a better service for their customers: the children. There is no room for narcissism and egos – and certainly no room for the power-hungry. Over the past twenty-five years, I have seen government reforms that continually place more pressure on teachers, and new ideas and exams systems that just provide more obstacles to schools, not only in terms of workload, but also in the financial costs of training and materials, which in many cases are published well after the courses have started.

Inspectorates themselves are accountable for introducing inspections not in the best interests of the children they serve, but data-driven and lacking support and empathy for the teachers. Ofsted set up a framework built fundamentally on data to prove results, and the constant teaching to the next set of tests has not only created work and distress for teachers, it has encouraged unethical practice in state schools desperate to maintain their league table status. It has also allowed unfair practice for those schools in areas where competition for places is high. I have seen first-hand blatant misreporting of exam results in the local press, which is neither transparent, honest nor ethical. How many children have also been sacrificed by not being permitted to continue into Year 13 to take their final exams because their first-year exam results were poor? It is quite common for pupils to progress rapidly in the last year before their final exams and achieve their target results, and yet schools are prepared to deny this opportunity to the children in their care in fear that their results will suffer. The temptation is understandable because it's not just the league tables that schools have to worry about; our world also has international, immediate and potentially damaging social media platforms open to anyone who has an opinion on education, whether well- or ill-informed – and well- or ill-intentioned.

A truly effective school is one that provides added value for the individual and I hope this new framework is a step in the right direction.

The new Ofsted framework comprises four sections:

- quality of education
- behaviour and attitudes
- personal development
- leadership and management

Quality of education

The quality of education section is split into three parts:

Intent

- To create a curriculum that is ambitious and fully inclusive.
- To offer a broad and rich curriculum for as long as possible (avoid curriculum narrowing too soon).
- Has the same ambitions for all learners.
- To ensure that the curriculum delivers cultural capital which is the 'essential knowledge that pupils need to be educated citizens, introducing them to the best that has been thought and said and helping to engender an appreciation of human creativity and achievement'.

Implementation

- To ensure that teachers have expert knowledge and, if not, they supported in this.
- For teachers to present information clearly and encourage appropriate discussion.
- Check pupils' understanding and correct misunderstandings with clear and direct feedback.
- Ensure key concepts are stored in long-term memory and not simply memorised as disconnected facts.
- Create an environment focused on learning.
- A rigorous approach to reading.

Impact

- Ensure learners develop a detailed knowledge across the curriculum for future learning.
- Success that meets national expectations is reflected in national tests and exams.
- Preparing pupils for the next stage of education, training or employment.

The quality of education section focuses on setting high expectations for all pupils, ensuring a fully inclusive and demanding curriculum. Teachers are expected to understand the age groups they teach and the needs of the individual. Teachers should be able to call on previous and current assessment to ensure progression and plan effective teaching and learning strategies. The curriculum should provide equal opportunities and address key literacy, numeracy and ICT concepts and developments. The curriculum at KS3 in particular should be sufficiently demanding and focus on reading, writing and oral communication. The new framework defines spiritual, moral, social and cultural development and how this is embedded into the curriculum and school life in general

Behaviour and attitudes

- To provide a safe, calm, orderly and positive environment and classroom setting.
- To set clear routines and expectations.
- To be punctual and encourage good attendance.

- Create an environment of mutual respect where learners are committed to learning.
- An environment of positive attitudes.

Personal development

- To embrace British values of democracy, individual liberty, the rule of law, and mutual respect and tolerance.
- A culture of equality in the classroom.
- To develop an all-inclusive environment.
- Opportunities to develop confidence, resilience and knowledge.
- The safe use of mobile devices.
- To be reflective.
- To have knowledge of and respect for people's feelings and values.
- To develop a fascination for learning.
- To embrace imagination and creativity.
- Within the leadership and management requirements is the overarching resonance of setting high expectations and a focus on the outcomes for pupils.

Taking into consideration the new Ofsted framework, the ISI framework, and revisiting the original forms used in 2014, the Stage 1 form for 2019/20 has been adapted yet again as below.

The Stage 1 foci should be relevant to your school. You may know of a particular area the school needs to focus on, or there might need to be specific age-related foci such as in the junior school, reading aloud, singing, and a focus on phonics and the correct pronunciation of words. This new form has links to the foci of both frameworks and, although only suggestions, your foci can be linked directly to a particular aspect of the framework if that is where your concerns or desire for improvement lies.

When one compares the frameworks more closely, the Ofsted framework embraces the emotional environment far more effectively than the ISI framework, which now appears rather formulaic and cold, almost lacking in the human factor. Therefore, there is much more reference to the Ofsted framework in our new form because the emotional environment still remains our primary focus. The Ofsted framework also captures the 'wow factor', the awe and wonder we want pupils to experience in the classroom through developing a fascination for learning and embracing imagination and creativity.

Table 12.1 Emotional environment of the classroom

Emotional Environment of the classroom	ISI/Ofsted
The lesson begins on time	Behaviour and attitudes
The register is taken	Behaviour and attitudes
There are high expectations of behaviour	Behaviour and attitudes, P4, P5
The teacher is aware of pupil activity throughout the room	Quality of education
The classroom environment is positive, friendly and welcoming	Behaviour and attitudes, personal development and quality of Education
The teacher uses positive communication and praise	Behaviour and attitudes
The teacher is active and works the room. (where able/appropriate)	Behaviour and attitudes, personal development
The teacher encourages plenty of positive eye contact and individual recognition	Behaviour and attitudes, quality of education
The classroom is a safe, calm, orderly and positive setting conducive to focussed learning	Behaviour and attitudes
There is an environment of mutual respect and a commitment to learning	Behaviour and attitudes, A8
Pupils' attitudes are aspirational	Personal development

Table 12.2 The nuts and bolts

The nuts and bolts	Yes/No/Notes
Pupils are aware of the lessons' learning objectives	Quality of education
There is evidence of progression from the last lesson in the learning objectives	Quality of education
The pace and content of the lesson is challenging for all pupils	Quality of education
Pupils' learning is enhanced by clear engagement and active participation	P1, P2 A3, behaviour and attitudes, personal development
The lesson is fully inclusive of all pupils with clear evidence of differentiation	Quality of education
Prior knowledge, skills and understanding is evidence through effective questioning	A2, A6, A8, quality of education, personal development

Table 12.2 Cont.

The nuts and bolts	Yes/No/Notes
Effective differentiation allows all pupils to progress	P5, P1, quality of education
Questioning extends and challenges pupils	P1, A3, A6, A8, quality of education
Communication is developed through a variety of speaking, listening and writing tasks	A2, A3, A6, A8, behaviour and attitudes, personal development
The teacher presents information clearly and encourages appropriate discussion	Quality of education
Teacher knowledge is excellent and clearly communicated	Quality of education
Incorrect understating nor misunderstandings is challenged with direct feedback	Quality of education
Key concepts are taught for long - term memory in context and not memorised as disconnected facts	Quality of education

Table 12.3 Independence

The Independence	
Pupils show good progress by setting their own success criteria	P1, P2, P5, A8, Personal Development
Self-assessment provides opportunities for reflection and improvement	P1, P4, A8, Behaviour and Attitudes, Quality of Education, Personal Development
Collaborative learning enhances attitudes to learning	P5, A8, Behaviour and Attitudes, Quality of Education
Independence is promoted through opportunities in the classroom	P1, P2, A6, A8, Behaviour and Attitudes, Personal Development

Table 12.4 Technical

The Technical	
Pupils use ICT effectively	A2, A5, A8, quality of education, personal development
There is evidence of numeracy challenges in non-mathematical lessons	A2, A4, A8, quality of education, personal development
Pupils are encouraged to read	Quality of education
Pupils and teachers select and determine appropriate use of ICT, visual aids and opportunities for practical activities	A5, A6, A3, A8, P2
There is attention to literacy	Quality of education A2, A3

Table 12.5 The wow factor

The Wow factor	
There is an element of "awe and wonder"	Personal development
Pupils are motivated by challenge and inspiration	P1, P3, P4, A8, dehaviour and attitudes, quality of education, personal development
Pupils are engaged by exciting and imaginative lessons	P5, A3, A8, behaviour and attitudes, quality of education
Pupils' attitudes are aspirational	P1, P2, P4, P5, A8,behaviour and attitudes, quality of education, personal development
Pupils are encouraged to take risks with their learning	Behaviour and attitudes, A8

Table 12.6 British values/SMSC

Evidence and reference to:
ISI regulatory compliance and focussed compliance inspection
• Part 1:2 SMSC • Part 2: P3, P4, P5, P6 and P7
Ofsted:
• Personal Development, Behaviour and Attitudes, evidence within the curriculum for Quality of Education

Pupil feedback form: senior school

Table 12.7 Pupil feedback form: senior school

	Strongly Agree	Agree	Disagree	Strongly Disagree
Emotional Environment				
My lesson is on time				
My classmates behave appropriately in this lesson				
I enjoy/look forward to this lesson				
My teacher is enthusiastic about this subject				
The classroom is a positive, friendly and welcome place to be				
There is an environment of mutual respect and a commitment to learning				
I can ask for help if I need it				
The Nuts and Bolts				
I am able to learn in this lesson				
I feel positively challenged in this lesson				
My teacher explains the topic, clearly and concisely				
We do a range of tasks in this lesson				
My teacher assigns regular prep/coursework/ independent work				
My teacher regularly marks my work				
I feel that I am making good progress				
I feel I am understanding as a learner				
This was a typical (normal or usual) lesson				

Pupil feedback form: junior school

Table 12.8 Pupil feedback form: junior school

	Strongly Agree	Agree	Disagree	Strongly Disagree
Emotional Environment				
My lesson is on time				
My classmates behave appropriately in this lesson				
I enjoy/look forward to this lesson				
My teacher is enthusiastic about this subject				
The classroom is a friendly and happy place to be				
Everyone wants to learn				
I can ask for help if I need it				
The Nuts and Bolts				
I am able to learn in this lesson				
I always have enough work to do				
The lessons are really interesting				
I am set work to do on my own in school and/or at home				
I feel that I am making good progress				
I feel I am understood as a learner				
This was a typical (normal or usual) lesson				

▮Teacher feedback form: senior school

Table 12.9 Teacher feedback form: senior school

	Strongly Agree	*Agree*	*Disagree*	*Strongly Disagree*
Emotional Environment				
My lesson is on time				
Behaviour in the classroom is excellent				
I enjoy/look forward to this lesson				
The classroom is a positive, friendly and welcome place to be				
There is an environment of mutual respect and a commitment to learning				
The Nuts and Bolts				
Pupils learn well in this lesson				
I look forward to this lesson				
I positively challenge in this lesson				
I feel pupils are making good progress in this lesson				
I use a range of tasks in this lesson				
I set regular prep/coursework/independent work				
I regularly mark pupils' work				
I understand my pupils as learners				
This was a typical (normal or usual) lesson				

What would we expect to see from the results?

This is a fictional set of results but in line with what one would expect after a couple of years – if not before.

Building the statements

Drawing on evidence across the school from the observations, it is relatively easy to write freely and confidently a concise and accurate self-reflection of what is going on in your school. Whoever undertakes the Stage 1 observations could file away under each section the evidence observed.

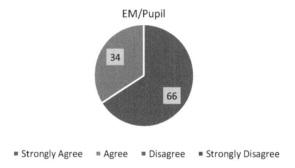

Figure 12.1 Emotional environment: pupil

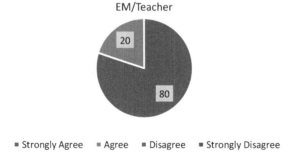

Figure 12.2 Emotional environment: teacher

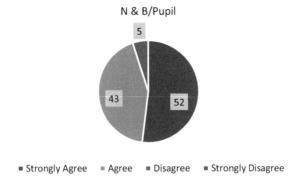

Figure 12.3 Nuts and bolts: pupil

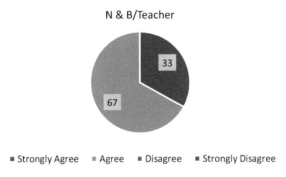

Figure 12.4 Nuts and bolts: teacher

Brief example for A4: numeracy (ISI)

Apart from the obvious mathematics courses…

> *Creative arts subjects develop numeracy skills through teaching perspective and ratio, photography with shutter speed and aperture, and modern foreign languages that employ counting games. Music promotes numeracy through rhythms and complex time signatures, food technology with measuring and quantities, and DT employing estimation of areas and volumes. The Stage 1 lesson observation includes numeracy as an area of focus and teachers actively promote its use in the majority of lessons.*

Brief example for A8: attitudes (ISI)

Evidence from the Stage 1 lesson observations show that attitudes to learning across the school are excellent. Pupils are attentive, focused and eager to grasp new concepts. 95% of lesson feedback from pupils shows that they enjoy the learning environment and appreciate the effort and expertise of teachers, as well as the variety of class-based activities. Lessons across the school provide opportunities for collaborative group work, such as the Year 8 composition task on minimalism, and opportunities for independent study, such as research on Brexit for debate in English classes. 97% of pupils feel positively challenged and enjoy their lessons. Work is regularly marked and pupils are keen to share their results and suggestions for improvements with others.

Brief example for implementation: developing understanding, not memorising disconnected facts (Ofsted)

Evidence from the Stage 1 observations shows that, across all subjects, previous learning and factual learning is embedded within a wider understanding of the topic. For example, in Year 12 history, the module on strategy pulls across previous learning of different war strategies, and compares and contrasts points in time and similarities in conflicts. In music, the use of Italian terms and dynamics are embedded into composition work and discussed as compositional development, recalling meanings and their uses. Pupils recall facts from a recent art project as part of the composition project and can accurately place artists and musicians in time and compare minimalist styles. In Year 9, during geography lessons, pupils confidently recall facts from the coastal field trip to explore further the topic of erosion, and compare and contrast data from other sources and coastlines.

Brief example for behaviour and attitudes: environment (Ofsted)

Stage 1 lesson observations provide quantitative feedback that pupils feel their classrooms are positive learning environments. 94% of pupils across the school feel the classroom is friendly and there is an atmosphere of mutual respect. 80% of pupils feel that behaviour in the classroom is good, but this is an area for more focus as the percentage is lower than the school's expectations. Teacher feedback is comparable with pupil feedback showing there is a mutual and accurate understanding of what takes place during lessons that are typical throughout the year.

Example for P8: pupils' knowledge and understanding of how to stay safe and be physically and mentally happy

The LV4Life programme's (PSHE) curriculum embraces all aspects of emotional, mental and physical well-being. Dedicated lessons give pupils the opportunity to debate and discuss pertinent and often sensitive subjects in a safe and caring environment where pupils feel able to contribute freely without judgement and receive mutual respect and understanding from their peers. This is evidenced through structured lesson observations as part of the three-stage lesson observation programme.

The data collected from the three-stage lesson observation programme is invaluable in that it is fresh, direct from the horse's mouth and an accurate reflection of the school. Overall, what better way to gain a clear and unbiased view of the performance of your school?

What's next?

This chapter reflects on the impact of the COVID-19 pandemic and how the three-stage lesson observation programme can be applied to online lessons.

The advent of the global pandemic meant normal routines and practices virtually disappeared overnight. Our school was in the early stages of a three-year programme to develop more flipped and blended learning – a new learning journey. The first lockdown, forcing the move to online learning immediately, accelerated the process and all the issues accompanying this learning transformation, one of those being lesson observation and how the programme might have to adapt – if at all. This chapter looks at the challenges of maintaining a healthy emotional environment in the classroom when working remotely.

More than ever, we need to be part of lessons and to know that the emotional environment, whether face-to-face or online, is what it should be. Online learning does not need to be clinical; indeed, blended learning and face-to-face time online are extremely rewarding, and pupil outcomes could be even better due to more individualised and self-directed learning. What pupils will need is a positive learning environment with increased empathy and support, as well as the teacher's ability to bring the class together when physically they can't be. Mental health issues in children were – and continue to be – widely reported as a direct impact of lockdown and remote learning, and the emotional environment of lessons, including online, cannot be underestimated.

Teams, Zoom and other platforms can facilitate assemblies, tutor group sessions, PSHE lessons and other mental health initiatives, all key to support pupils, staff and parents during this unprecedented time.

During the first lockdown, I was added to every class Microsoft 365 Team across the school. This wasn't Big Brother watching, as such, but to show my support and commitment as a leader. I could, if I wished, pop into any of the lessons that were going on. I know this was not seen as a threat because our open-door culture, and unannounced lesson observations had paved the way for total trust and transparency. Staff were eager for senior leaders, myself included, to comment on the Team chat here and there, to show the children we were still engaged with them even though they were not in school. Children found it very funny that sometimes I would inadvertently turn up to their lesson when I had clicked the wrong invitation. The best example of this was when I should have been with the executive committee of the Licensed Trade Charity (our umbrella organisation) but turned up in a Year 10 philosophy lesson. I'm not sure who was more surprised, but it created a genuine sense of fun, laughter and comedy. The children abso-lutely loved it, one cheeky chap adding, 'Ma'am, next time can you warn us you are coming – you scared us!' The sense of fun and well-being is what it was about. The emotional environment within the lesson, even when online, means so much to staff and pupils if senior leaders get it right.

A TES article (Gibbons 2020) quoted Mary Bousted, joint general secretary of the NEU teaching union, stating that 'schools carrying out performance management observations while they are closed to the majority of pupils have "completely failed to understand" that education should be done dif-ferently during the Covid-19 crisis'. This is so correct. The fact that both ISI and Ofsted were looking to start inspections again in January 2021, unless there was a safeguarding focus for the welfare of pupils, is unforgiveable. Looking ahead at the uncertainty of coronavirus variants and further dis-ruption, I would find any form of classroom inspection disappointing. But it doesn't mean schools can't support their staff through positive experiences to build confidence again, especially with renewed technology, through the Stage 1 observations.

However, throughout, the focus of the TES article is the link with per-formance appraisal, which so incredibly sad. If the lesson observations were decoupled from performance appraisal, we would be celebrating the amazingly innovative and creative approach teachers have applied to pro-viding remote, flipped and blended learning. There are many teachers who would jump at the chance to share their good practice. If we had pooled our resources and shared good practice, morale among staff would be higher and the well-being of our sector safeguarded during a period of time when the teaching profession has been slated in the press.

Why should education be done differently during the COVID-19 crisis? If we had got it right with technology and 21st-century teaching and learning while in school, the impact would not have been so disastrous.

I believe our school's ability to pull it off during lockdown was primarily due to the emotional environment within the school and the genuine camaraderie among staff to give the best to their pupils, putting their own needs second. This emotional environment and care continued throughout school closure and no one felt abandoned.

There is no reason why the three-stage lesson observation programme has to change to adapt to adverse conditions such as the pandemic. Human good nature, empathy and understanding are the same whether you are face-to-face in class with pupils, talking to them on a screen or writing in chat facilities. There are still expectations around planning and delivery, report writing and assessment, even if the policies and procedures change to adapt for flipped, blended or remote learning. Staff contributions might not necessarily be contact sports or singing activities at the moment, but staff can be flexible in what they offer and adapt accordingly. Contribution is contribution whatever its any form.

Education will not be the same following the pandemic. This is the perfect opportunity to re-evaluate our teaching practices and deliver for the 21st century. What doesn't change, though, is the emotional environment around learning. In fact, it is even more important now as we move to a more blended approach and, undoubtedly, more remote learning. Children and staff need our empathy and understanding. With empathy, understanding and a secure emotional environment, teaching practices will get better and better as confidence rises, and along with it the outcomes for pupils will soar. Teachers are on a significant learning journey – we are in it together.

In conclusion

An emotionally secure school can face any challenge now and in the future.

There is nothing more terrifying than taking on the culture of a new school, or indeed, one you inherited. Each school culture is unique and has formed over a long period of time, and nearly all will have their abundance of storytellers to keep the fable going, like most traditions. Only you as leader can ascertain what that culture is and whether it needs to change. It may be that, overall, the culture is very positive and productive, but the fear of lesson observation and being held to account is still the elephant in the room. To improve the quality of teaching and learning, and pupil outcomes, to take away the fear of being observed and inadvertently changing the school culture can surely only be positive. All you need to do is:

- Explore what the culture currently is.
- Understand yourself.
- Understand your team.
- Determine the effectiveness of teaching and learning.
- Determine the foci for the observation forms.
- Prepare the paperwork and policies.
- Plan introducing the programme to team and staff.
- Be brave, confident and decisive.
- Be prepared to reflect but not relinquish.
- Enjoy the change and see your school transform.

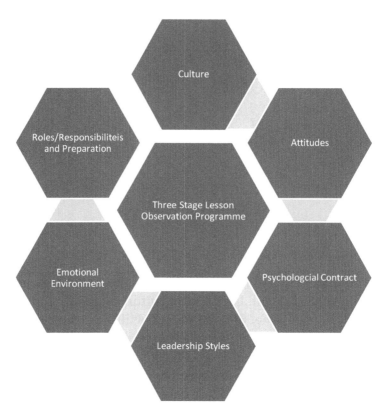

Figure 14.1 Summary

References

Allen, M. (2014) 'Graded lesson observations are a major cause of stress for FE teachers'. The Guardian, 11 June 2014. www.theguardian. com/education/2014/jun/11/graded-lesson-observations-stress-teachers-further-education

Al-Malki, M. and Juan, M. (2018) 'Leadership Styles and Job Performance: A Literature Review'. *Journal of International Business Research and Marketing*, Vol. 3 (3), 40–49

Amanchukwu, R.N., Stanley, G.J. and Ololube, N.P. (2015) 'A Review of Leadership Theories, Principles and Styles and Their Relevance to Educational Management'. *Management*, Vol. 5 (1), 6–14

AQR International (2017) 'ILM72'. AQR International, 11 May 2017. https:// aqrinternational.co.uk/integrated-leadership-measure-ilm72

AQR International (2017) 'MTQ48'. AQR International, 11 May 2017. https:// aqrinternational.co.uk/product/mtq48-assessment

Aritzeta, A., Swales, S. and Senior, B. (2007) 'Belbin's Team Role Model: Development, Validity and Applications for Team Building'. *Journal of Management Studies*, Vol. 44 (1), 96–118

Bell, G. (2013) 'Teamwork makes the team work: an interview with Dr Meredith Belbin'. *Human Resource Management International Digest*, Vol. 21 (2) 45–47

Blancero, D., Marron, G. and Keller, T. (1997) 'Managing Psychological Contracts'. *Employment Relations Today*, Vol. 24 (2), 1–10

Bennis, W. (1999) 'The Leadership Advantage'. *Leader to Leader*, Vol. 1999 (12), 18–23

Branson, R. (2011) 'Virgin's Richard Branson: Apple boss Steve Jobs was the entrepreneur I most admired'. The Telegraph, 6 October 2011. www.telegraph.co.uk/technology/steve-jobs/8811232/Virgins-Richard-Branson-Apple-boss-Steve-Jobs-was-the-entrepreneur-I-most-admired.html

Brown, L.A., and Roloff, M.E. (2011) 'Extra-Role Time, Burnout, and Commitment: The Power of Promises Kept'. *Business and Professional Communication Quarterly*, Vol. 74 (4), 450–474

Choudhury, G. (2011) 'The Dynamics of Organizational Climate: An Exploration'. *Management Insight*, Vol. 7 (2), 111–116

Connor, T. (2016) 'Relationships: The Key to Student Engagement'. *International Journal of Education and Learning*, Vol. 5 (1), 13–22

Conway, N. and Briner, R.B. (2002) 'A Daily Diary Study of Affective Responses to Psychological Contract Breach and Exceeded Promises'. *Journal of Organizational Behavior*, Vol. 23 (3), 287–302

Conway, N. and Briner, R.B. (2005) *Understanding Psychological Contracts at Work: A Critical Evaluation of Theory and Research*. Oxford: Oxford University Press

Corradino, C. and Fogarty, K. (2016) 'Positive Emotions and Academic Achievement'. *Applied Psychology OPUS*, Vol. 7. https://wp.nyu.edu/steinhardt-appsych_opus/positive-emotions-and-academic-achievement/

Dix, P. (2017) *When the Adults Change, Everything Changes: Seismic Shifts in School Behaviour*. Bancyfelin, Wales: Independent Thinking Press

Elstad, E., Christopherson, K.A. and Turmo, A. (2011) 'Social Exchange Theory as an Explanation of Organizational Citizenship Behaviour among Teachers'. *International Journal of Leadership in Education: Theory and Practice*, Vol. 14 (4), 405–421

Erickson, F. (1987) 'Conceptions of School Culture: An Overview'. *Educational Administration Quarterly*, Vol. 23 (4), 11–24

Eyre, D. (2016) *High Performance Learning: How to Become a World Class School*. Routledge: Abingdon

Ferguson, D. (2018) 'I will never return to teach in England': the UK teachers finding refuge abroad'. The Guardian, 2 October 2018. www.theguardian.com/education/2018/oct/02/never-return-teach-england-refuge-abroad

Fisher, S.G., Hunter, T.A. and Macrosson, W.D.K. (2011) 'The Structure of Belbin's Team Roles'. *Journal of Occupational and Organizational Psychology*, Vol. 71 (3), 283–288

Forte, A. (2011) 'How Does Organizational Climate Influence the Ethical Behaviour of People in an Organization?' *International Business and Economics Research Journal*, Vol. 2 (10), 66–72

Francesco, A.M., Gold, B.A. (1998) *International Organizational Behavior*. New Jersey: Prentice Hall

George, C. (2009) *The Psychological Contract: Managing and Developing Professional Groups*. Maidenhead: McGraw Hill, Open University Press

George, G., Sleeth, R.G. and Siders, M.A. (1999) 'Organizing Culture: Leader Roles, Behaviors, and Reinforcement Mechanisms'. *Journal of Business and Psychology*, Vol. 13 (4) 545–560

Gibbons, A. (2020) 'Exclusive: Lockdown observations for 1 in 10 teachers'. TES online, 8 June 2020. www.tes.com/news/exclusive-lockdown-observations-1-10-teachers

Gilbert, I. (2018) *The Working Class: Poverty, Education and Alternative Voices*. Bancyfelin, Wales: Independent Thinking Press

Gosling, D. (2002) 'Models of Peer Observation of Teaching'. London: LTSN Generic Centre

Gosling, D. (2005) 'Peer observation of teaching'. London: Staff and Educational Development Association

Higgins-D'Alessandro, A. and Sadh, D. (1998) 'The Dimensions and Measurement of School Culture: Understanding School Culture as the Basis for School Reform'. *International Journal of Educational Research*, Vol. 27 (7), 553–569

Hofstede, G., Hofstede, G.J. and Minkov, M. (2010) *Cultures and Organizations: Software of the Mind*. New York: McGraw Hill

Horton, H. (2019) 'Britain's strictest school's first GCSE results are four times better than national average'. The Telegraph, 22 August 2019. www.telegraph.co.uk/news/2019/08/22/britains-strictest-schools-first-gcse-results-four-times-better/

Howes, K.L. (1993) 'Identifying, Defining a Leadership Style'. *National Association of Secondary School Principals Bulletin*, Vol. 77 (554), 55–62

Baldino, D. (2017) 'What is DISC?' IMS Technology Services, 10 August 2017. www.imsts.com/what-is-disc

ISC Research (2018) Global Report on the International Schools Market

Jazaieri, H. (2018) 'Compassionate Education from Preschool to Graduate School: Bringing a Culture of Compassion into the Classroom'. *Journal of Research in Innovative Teaching and Learning*, Vol. 11 (1), 22–66

Johns Hopkins Medical Institutions. (2008) 'Mendel Didn't Have The Whole Picture: Our Genome Changes Over Lifetime, Johns Hopkins Experts Say'. Johns Hopkins Medicine, 24 June 2008. www.hopkinsmedicine.org/news/media/releases/mendel_didnt_have_the_whole_picture_our_genome_changes_over_lifetime_johns_hopkins_experts_say

Khan, M.S., Khan, I., Eureshi, Q.A., Ismail, H.M., Rauf, H., Latif, A. and Tahir, M. (2015) 'The Styles of Leadership: A Critical Review'. *Public Policy and Administration Research*, Vol. 5 (3), 87–92

Kwan, P. (2009) 'Beginning Teachers' Perceptions of School Human Resource Practices'. *Asia Pacific Journal of Education*, Vol. 29 (3), 373–386

Lasagabaster, D. and Sierra, J.M. (2011) 'Classroom Observation: Desirable Conditions Established by Teachers'. *European Journal of Teacher Education*, Vol. 34 (4), 449–463

Linstead, S., Fulop, L. and Lilley, S. (2004) *Management and Organization*. Cheltenham: Palgrave Macmillan

Macrosson, W.D.K. and Hemphill, D.J. (2001) 'Machiavellianism in Belbin Team Roles'. *Journal of Managerial Psychology*, Vol. 16 (5), 355–364

Marshall, S. (1993) 'Managing the Culture: The Key to Effective Change'. *School Leadership and Management*, Vol. 13 (3), 255–268

Marston, W.M. (1928) *Emotions of Normal People*. London, UK: Routledge 1999

McGrath, J., Bates, B. (2013) *The Little Book of Big Management Theories…and how to use them*. (2nd edn) Harlow, UK: Pearson

Mercado, D. (2019) 'Ken Fisher's sexist comments have cost his company nearly $1 billion in assets'. NBR, 17 October 2019. http://nbr.com/2019/10/17/ken-fishers-sexist-comments-have-cost-his-company-nearly-1-billion-in-assets/

Meslec, N. and Curșeu, P.L. (2015) 'Are Balanced Groups Better? Belbin Roles in Collaborative Learning Groups'. *Learning and Individual Differences*, Vol. 39, 81–88

Minarik, M.M., Thornton, B., Perreault, G. (2003) 'Systems Thinking Can Improve Teacher Retention'. *The Clearing House: A Journal of Educational Strategies, Issues and Ideas*, Vol. 76 (5), 230–234

Nanjundeswaraswamy, T.S. and Swamy, D.R. (2014) 'Leadership Styles'. *Advances in Management*, Vol. 7 (2), 57–62

Owens, R.G. and Steinhoff, C.R. (1989) 'Towards a Theory of Organisational Culture'. *Journal of Educational Administration*, Vol. 27 (3)

Pellegrini, E.K. and Scandura, T.A. (2008) 'Paternalistic Leadership: A Review and Agenda for Future Research'. *Journal of Management*, Vol. 34 (3), 566–593

Petrides, K.V. (2010) 'Trait Emotional Intelligence Theory'. *Industrial and Organizational Psychology*, Vol. 3 (2), 136–139

Plomin, R. (2018) *Blueprint: How DNA Makes Us Who We Are*. London: Allen Lane

Price, H.E. (2011) 'Principal–Teacher Interactions: How Affective Relationships Shape Principal and Teacher Attitudes'. *Educational Administration Quarterly*, Vol. 48 (1), 39–85

Robinson, J. (2019) 'ISC response to Daily Telegraph article on future of independent schools'. Independent Schools Council, 13 September 2019. www.isc.co.uk/media-enquiries/news-press-releases-statements/isc-response-to-daily-telegraph-article-on-future-of-independent-schools/

Robinson, S.L., Morrison, E.W. (1995) 'Psychological Contracts and OCB: The Effect of Unfulfilled Obligations on Civic Virtue Behavior'. *Journal of Organizational Behavior*, Vol. 16 (3), 289–298

Sarason, S.B. (1971) *The Culture of the School and the Problem of Change.* Boston: Allyn and Bacon

Schein, E.H. (1985) *Organisational Culture and Leadership.* San Francisco: Jossey-Bass

Smircich, L. (1983) 'Concepts of Culture and Organisational Analysis'. *Administrative Science Quarterly*, Vol. 28 (3), 339–358

Smith, A. (1759) *The Theory of Moral Sentiments.* London: Printed for A. Millar, and A. Kincaid and J. Bell

Smith, P. (2013) 'Open up your classrooms: we need a new approach to lesson observations'. The Guardian, 24 July 2013. www.theguardian.com/teacher-network/teacher-blog/2013/jul/24/lesson-observations-new-approach-teaching-classroom

Stephens, T.L. (2015) 'Encouraging Positive Student Engagement and Motivation: Tips for Teachers'. Review360 Pearson, 21 August 2015. www.pearsoned.com/encouraging-positive-student-engagement-and-motivation-tips-for-teachers/

Suazo, M.M., Martinez, P.G., Sandoval, R. (2011) 'Creating Psychological and Legal Contracts through HRM Practices: A Strength of Signals Perspective'. *Employee Responsibilities and Rights Journal*, Vol. 23 (3), 187–204

Tekleab, A.G., Chiaburu, D.S. (2011) 'Social Exchange: Empirical Examination of Form and Focus'. *Journal of Business Research*, Vol. 64 (5), 460–466

Uzohue, C.E., Yaya, J.A., Akintayo, O.A. (2016) 'A Review of Leadership Theories, Principles and Styles and their Relevance to Management of Health Science Libraries in Nigeria'. *Journal of Educational Leadership and Policy*, Vol. 1 (1), 17–26

Wilsher, S. (2015) 'Behavior Profiling: Implications for Recruitment and Team Building'. *Strategic Direction*, Vol. 31 (9), 1–5

Woolcock, N. (2019) 'One in ten pupils off-rolled before GCSEs'. The Times, 11 October 2019. www.thetimes.co.uk/article/one-in-ten-pupils-off-rolled-before-gcses-3gbnh8l3r

Yasir, M., Imran, R., Kashif Irshad, M., Mohamad, N.A. and Khan, M.M. (2016) 'Leadership Styles in Relation to Employees' Trust and Organizational Change Capacity: Evidence From Non-Profit Organizations'. *Sage Open*, Vol. 6 (4)

Zaare, M. (2013) 'An Investigation into the Effect of Classroom Observation on Teaching Methodology'. *Procedia: Social and Behavioral Sciences*, Vol. 70, 605–614

Bibliography

Compton, M. (2016) 'The Role of Teaching Observations: Developing or Managing Academic Practice?" *Compass: Journal of Learning and Teaching*, Vol. 8 (12)

Engin, M. and Priest, B. (2014) 'Observing Teaching: A Lens for Self-Reflection', *Journal of Perspectives in Applied Academic Practice*, Vol. 2 (2), 2–9

Suazo, M. (2011) 'Implications of the Psychological Contract Breach'. *Journal of Management Psychology*, Vol. 26 (5), 366–382

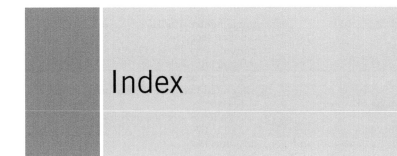

Index

Note: Page numbers in *italics* indicate figures, **bold** numbers indicate tables, on the corresponding pages.